ADSTRAT
AN ADVERTISING DECISION SUPPORT SYSTEM

INSTRUCTOR'S MANUAL
REVISED

by

Hubert Gatignon & Raymond R. Burke

THE WHARTON SCHOOL · UNIVERSITY OF PENNSYLVANIA

▲ *The Scientific Press*
651 Gateway Boulevard • Suite 1100 • South San Francisco, CA 94080-7014

ADSTRAT: AN ADVERTISING DECISION SUPPORT SYSTEM
INSTRUCTOR'S MANUAL REVISED
by Hubert Gatignon and Raymond R. Burke

Printed in the United States of America

10 9 8 7 6 5 4 3 2 1

ISBN 0-89426-221-1

Publisher: The Scientific Press
Text design & production editor: Gene Smith
Cover design by Rogondino & Associates

Cover photo © 1991. Geoff Smyth / ACE / Nawrocki Stock Photo, Inc.

CONTENTS

PREFACE

The ADSTRAT system reflects the authors' experience in teaching advertising courses at the undergraduate and graduate levels. The motivation for designing ADSTRAT came from two basic directions. First, we felt that the advertising course should focus on the decision-making process. This implied providing students with a set of tools (concepts, methods, and theories) to assist them in making advertising planning decisions. In addition, we wanted students to exercise this knowledge in an applied context, where the interrelationships between advertising decisions would become apparent. While this is typically achieved by asking students to design an advertising campaign for an existing product, we felt that this type of project typically did not provide students with sufficient information to adequately address the problem. ADSTRAT was designed to overcome these limitations: to provide students with a rich experience in advertising planning and to encourage them to apply marketing science techniques in the evaluation of advertising alternatives.

ADSTRAT is the result of several years of work and multiple adaptations. A few of the current ADSTRAT options were developed by the first author on a mainframe computer. Students were supplied with datasets of background information and were asked to use the computer tools, along with existing statistical analysis software, to develop an advertising campaign. Unfortunately, the lack of integration of the various modules and the complexity of the software proved to be a major hindrance to the learning process. The instructor was forced to spend a considerable amount of class time on computer instruction, and this distracted from the discussion of advertising issues.

Technological changes presented the opportunity to develop an integrated advertising decision support system on the personal computer. The authors worked together to provide these resources to students in an easy-to-use package, and to include additional facilities for assisting advertising planning decisions. This concept was enriched considerably by the second author's research in the areas of artificial intelligence and expert systems.

The implementation of the initial ideas went through many refinements which benefited from the feedback of our students. The final ADSTRAT product is the fruit of a joint effort by the authors, their programmers (Paul Reber, Gang Shao, Shenjie Guan, and Michel Wilson), and research assistants (James Mendelsohn, Stephen Pessagno, and Eugene Rhee). We gratefully acknowledge the contributions of everyone involved.

Hubert Gatignon
Raymond R. Burke
July 1992

ADSTRAT SOFTWARE

The ADSTRAT PC-based software system provides the advertising or brand manager, account executive, or market researcher with an integrated set of tools and data for assisting a broad range of advertising management decisions. The system takes the user through the various stages of advertising planning, including situation analysis, setting the objectives, budgeting, creative strategy, and media planning.

Student Edition. The version of ADSTRAT supplied with this manual provides datasets designed especially for educational purposes.

Professional Edition. A professional version of ADSTRAT is available which provides additional utilities for accessing multiple data banks from specific industries, so that advertisers can have a comprehensive system for developing a brand's communication program.

1

Introduction

ADSTRAT provides instructors and students with an integrated set of tools and data for assisting advertising management decisions. By making these facilities available in a user-friendly package, ADSTRAT helps students to understand and use scientific techniques for advertising decision making. We felt that the advertising planner should not need an advanced degree in computer science, statistics, or mathematics to apply marketing science concepts and methods. Therefore, ADSTRAT was designed to allow non-technical users to evaluate advertising alternatives and justify their decisions with a minimum of effort. At the same time, sophisticated users will appreciate ADSTRAT's flexibility for representing marketing phenomena and investigating advertising issues.

It should be pointed out that (1) ADSTRAT is not a simulation of the effects of students' advertising decisions on consumer behavior, and (2) ADSTRAT does not automatically design an advertising campaign for students. Instead, the software should be viewed as a set of tools that students can use to better understand the market and competitive environment and to analyze a variety of key advertising decisions.

ADSTRAT can be used in a variety of advertising and communications classes, including undergraduate and graduate courses in advertising principles, communication principles, and advertising management. The software package can serve to expand the coverage of certain advertising concepts and methods in existing courses, or as the basis for a new course in advertising planning. It should be noted, however, that the ADSTRAT student manual was designed as a complement and not a substitute for an advertising textbook. It is assumed that the textbook discusses the field of advertising and the principles of advertising communication. ADSTRAT goes a step beyond this by enabling students to implement the theories, concepts, and analyses described in the textbook and class discussion in a practical decision-making context.

Most students have been exposed to a considerable amount of advertising. They are therefore inclined to base their advertising decision on personal knowledge and intuition rather than on communication theories and marketing science concepts (e.g., We should use a celebrity presenter and humor in this beer commercial because the approach was successful for brand X). To overcome this tendency, the ADSTRAT system does not use an existing brand, product, or industry. Instead, it provides detailed information about a new and unfamiliar market (Sonites). Students must rely on the data and their analyses to guide their advertising decisions. The market and competitive data were generated by the MARKSTRAT market simulation program. The consumer data were developed separately to conform to the MARKSTRAT environment. The media data reflect the actual cost and coverage of major print and broadcast vehicles. When taken together, these datasets represent the kinds of information typically available to advertising decision makers.

SYSTEM REQUIREMENTS

The ADSTRAT system was designed to run on any IBM-compatible personal computer. The software requires a minimum of one 3½" disk drive or two 5¼" disk drives. The software can be copied to a hard disk, if available. Although a color monitor and/or math coprocessor will enhance ADSTRAT's operation, they are not required.

For the installation procedure, please refer to the Appendix of the ADSTRAT manual.

Do You Have Problems in Installing ADSTRAT?

What is the problem?

ADSTRAT requires either ANSI.SYS or ANSI.COM to be installed on the computer you are using, either your personal computer or in a PC Lab. If one of these programs is not loaded, ADSTRAT will appear to display random characters on your screen. Though ADSTRAT will run, it will not display its results in a comprehensible manner.

How to fix the problem?

If you are using your own computer, it is simplest to change the configuration, i.e., to add a line in the CONFIG.SYS file. This procedure is described in the student manual's appendix, STEP 3. Install the ANSI.SYS Driver (p. 151).

If you are using a computer on a network, it is easier to run a program which will install the driver for as long as the computer is on. The ANSI.COM file required for this operation could not be included with the ADSTRAT manual because it is a public domain utility file which cannot be sold. However, the diskette supplied with the instructor's manual contains two files which will resolve your problem.

Copy these two files (ADST.BAT and ANSI.COM) onto your ADSTRAT floppy disk, change to the drive with the ADSTRAT disk, and type ADST.

That's it.

You can make these files available to your students so that they can use the procedure described above. The most convenient way is to have the students access the files (ADST.BAT and ANSI.COM) through a network. The handout included at the end of this chapter (Exhibit 1.1) can be adapted to give directions to the students on how to proceed. Note that ADSTRAT itself should not be used from a network. This is a violation of the licensing agreement.

FEATURES OF ADSTRAT

- Analysis modules are grouped together by advertising decision. ADSTRAT provides a range of tools from elementary to sophisticated so that students can start with a simple analysis, discover the limitations, and then move to more advanced tools.

- The interactive system brings to life data and models which receive insufficient or inaccessible coverage in advertising textbooks. ADSTRAT allows the instructor to demonstrate a variety of decision-making approaches using different methods and datasets.

- ADSTRAT uses a familiar menu bar and template format to minimize system learning time. It provides default datasets and options for all analysis tools. Class discussion can focus on the advertising issues rather than on the operational details of the user interface and data access.

- The student can switch between views of system input and output with a single keystroke, encouraging what-if analyses.

- The software illustrates a number of important advertising concepts including advertising response functions, communication models, psychographic research, positioning, reach and frequency, and marginal analysis.

CONTENT OF THE INSTRUCTOR'S MANUAL

The purpose of the Instructor's Manual is to suggest how the ADSTRAT system can be incorporated into the advertising course and presented to students. To this end, we provide two example syllabi, a project description, and a set of transparency masters which the instructor can use to introduce ADSTRAT to the class.

The ADSTRAT student manual discusses the statistical techniques and models used in the software package. Therefore, we do not repeat the discussion here. Instructors interested in more details about these techniques are referred to the literature cited in the ADSTRAT student manual. It is also not our intention in this manual to provide solutions for the advertising decisions presented by the ADSTRAT system. The instructor's objective in using ADSTRAT should not be to have students reach a specific answer, but to provide students with a scientific basis for exploring alternatives and justifying their decisions.

———————— **Exhibit 1.1** ————————

Example of Handout to Students to Download Fix Files from a Network

Running ADSTRAT in Wharton's PC Labs

What's The Problem?

ADSTRAT™ requires either ANSI.SYS or ANSI.COM to be installed. Neither one is installed in the Wharton PC Labs, and they might not be installed on your home PC. If one of these programs is not loaded, when you run ADSTRAT it will appear as if your computer has gone berserk. Though ADSTRAT will run, it will not display its results in a comprehensible manner.

Getting the Fix Files

To remedy this situation, take a formatted diskette (either Double Density 5¼" or Double or High Density 3½") to one of the Wharton PC Labs (116 SH/DH, 202-203 SH/DH, 210 VH). Don't place the diskette in any drive yet. Turn the computer off and back on to get to the Main Menu.

At the *Wharton Main Menu*, type NETWORK and press the Enter key (↵).

The *Wharton Network Menu* should appear. At this menu, type DOWNLOAD and press the Enter key (↵).

The *Wharton Download Menu* will appear. Select MRKT224 to download the appropriate ADSTRAT files. You will be asked to specify a disk drive. Put your diskette in the appropriate drive and select it on the screen. The files will be copied to your diskette. Press the Escape key when you're finished and turn off the computer when you are done.

Using the Fix Files

Copy the files you just downloaded onto the ADSTRAT floppy disk. Now you're ready to run ADSTRAT, either in the Wharton PC Labs or on your computer at home.

Change the directory to the floppy drive, and type ADST.

That's it.

2

Incorporating ADSTRAT into
the Advertising Course

ADSTRAT is an important instructional tool, but it should not be used without the support of additional readings and discussion. In teaching the advertising course, we often use a balanced combination of lectures, discussions, computer demonstrations, case studies, and reading materials. These pedagogical approaches are complementary, and together create an effective learning environment.

Students are typically given the assignment of designing an advertising campaign for one of the Sonite brands in the ADSTRAT data base (see Table 2.1 of the student manual). Several variations on this assignment are possible. One approach is to ask all of the students in a class to develop an advertising plan for the same brand, either individually or in groups. This facilitates the comparison of the final projects. If students present their campaigns to the class at the end of the course, this can stimulate a lively discussion of alternative advertising strategies and tactics. An additional advantage of this assignment is that the instructor can change the assigned brand over time and across classes to minimize the amount of information transmitted from one class of students to the next.

Another approach is to assign different Sonite brands to different students or groups. This can be especially interesting for the class if the assigned brands potentially compete for the same market segment. Following the ad campaign presentations, students can be asked to evaluate which brands are most likely to succeed in the market.

There are two basic ways to integrate the ADSTRAT assignment into the curriculum. The first is to cover the traditional advertising material in the first part of the course and then devote the second section to the advertising planning project (see Syllabus A in Exhibit 2.1). The ADSTRAT project provides an integrative experience, enabling students to apply the advertising concepts, theories, and models discussed in the first part. Alternatively, the instructor can ask students to complete sections of the advertising plan as each of the topics is covered in class (see Syllabus B in Exhibit 2.2). In this case, students are given feedback throughout the course, and can revise their decisions for the final written and/or verbal report due at the end of the class.

If the first method is chosen, the ADSTRAT system should, nevertheless, be introduced early in the class so that students can begin experimenting with the software and formulating an approach to the various planning decisions. It is helpful to demonstrate the various ADSTRAT options as topics are covered in class so that students learn the relationships between the advertising concepts and theories and the corresponding decision support methodologies. This also minimizes the information overload that can occur when the discussion of ADSTRAT is postponed until the end of the course.

The second approach is illustrated by Syllabus B. In this case, a heavier emphasis is placed on using ADSTRAT both within and outside of the classroom. The instructor will often spend significant amounts of class time describing and demonstrating ADSTRAT's modules for each advertising decision. Students are required to work on sections of the advertising planning project throughout the course and submit intermediate reports. Using the instructor's feedback, students can refine their final ad campaigns.

Each of these methods has potential advantages. The first method allows the instructor to place greater emphasis on conceptual and theoretical discussions of advertising issues. It also requires less integration of the ADSTRAT system with existing course material. The second approach places a greater emphasis on decision making. Students can potentially learn more about the application of ADSTRAT's methods because they are given feedback throughout the course. The continual interaction with ADSTRAT can also increase students' involvement and interest in the course.

In either case, we have found it valuable to introduce ADSTRAT as part of the objectives and requirements of the course in the first session. This establishes the decision-making orientation of the course and creates appropriate expectations concerning the demands of the advertising planning project. We distribute the ADSTRAT Project Description (Exhibit 2.3) along with the course syllabus on the first day of class.

——————— Exhibit 2.1 ———————

SYLLABUS A

GENERAL DESCRIPTION

The major course objectives are:

- to familiarize students with the theories and concepts of behavioral science, management science, and advertising research that are relevant to the job of advertising management;
- to enable students to apply this material to the decisions of an advertising or brand manager; and
- to encourage the development of oral and written presentation skills.

COURSE FORMAT AND CONTENT

The course is based on lectures, the discussion of cases and supplementary readings, and an advertising planning project. The course is divided into four major segments.

1. Advertising planning
2. Consumer analysis and setting advertising objectives
3. Budgeting and media planning
4. Creating advertising campaigns and measuring their effectiveness

COURSE REQUIREMENTS

Students must keep up with the reading schedule to participate in class discussions and be prepared for the exam. (Work on the group project may require that students read ahead of schedule.) In addition to regular reading assignments, the following are required:

Final group project report	50%
Exam	30%
Class participation	20%
	100%

Students will work in teams on an advertising plan for a brand assigned from ASTRAT. At the end of the course, each team will turn in a typed final report (not to exceed 20 double-spaced pages plus exhibits) consisting of a well-integrated and carefully documented proposal for an advertising campaign. No late projects will be accepted. Additional details are given in the attached document.

Exhibit 2.1

(continued)

SESSION
NUMBER   TOPICS

        I. *Advertising Planning*

1   Introduction: Overview of the Course and the ASTRAT System
2   Issues in Advertising Management: The Advertising Plan

      II. *Consumer Analysis and Setting Advertising Objectives*

3   Target Audience Selection and Profiling; ASTRAT Demonstration
4   Communication Objectives; ASTRAT Demonstration
5   Case #1 Discussion
6   Image and Competitive Position; ASTRAT Demonstration
7   Case #2 Discussion

     III. *Budgeting and Media Planning*

8   Budgeting; ASTRAT Demonstration
9   Media Selection
10   Media Planning Models; ASTRAT Demonstration
11   Exam

     IV. *Creating Advertising Campaigns and Measuring their Effectiveness*

12   Creative Strategy
13   Selecting Creative Tactics; ASTRAT Demonstration
14   Case #3 Discussion
15   Case #4 Discussion
16   Measuring Advertising Effectiveness
17   Case #5 Discussion

      V. *Other Topics*

18   Social/Economic Effects of Advertising
19   GROUP PRESENTATIONS
20   GROUP PRESENTATIONS
          GROUP PROJECT REPORT DUE: THE ADVERTISING CAMPAIGN

Exhibit 2.2

SYLLABUS B

GENERAL DESCRIPTION

The major course objectives are:

- to familiarize students with the theories and concepts of behavioral science, management science, and advertising research that are relevant to the job of advertising management;
- to enable students to apply this material to the decisions of an advering or brand manager; and
- to encourage the development of oral and written presentation skills.

COURSE FORMAT AND CONTENT

The course is based on lectures, the discussion of cases and supplementary readings, and an advertising planning project. The course is divided into four major segments.

1. Advertising planning
2. Consumer analysis and setting advertising objectives
3. Budgeting and media planning
4. Creating advertising campaigns and measuring their effectiveness

COURSE REQUIREMENTS

Students must keep up with the reading schedule to participate in class discussions and be prepared for the exam. (Work on the group project may require that students read ahead of schedule.) In addition to regular reading assignments, the following are required:

Group project report (part 1)	10%
Group project report (part 2)	10%
Final group project report	40%
Exam	20%
Class participation	20%
	100%

Students will work in teams on an advertising plan for a brand assigned from ASTRAT. Two intermediate project reports are due during the course of the term. Groups will be given feedback on these reports which can be used to refine the final campaign proposal. At the end of the course, each team will turn in a typed final report (not to exceed 20 double-spaced pages plus exhibits) consisting of a well-integrated and carefully documented proposal for an advertising campaign. No late projects will be accepted. Additional details are given in the attached document.

SESSION NUMBER	TOPICS
	I. *Advertising Planning*
1	Introduction: Overview of the Course and the ASTRAT System
2	Issues in Advertising Management: The Advertising Plan
	II. *Consumer Analysis and Setting Advertising Objectives*
3	Target Audience Selection and Profiling; ASTRAT Demonstration
4	Communication Objectives; ASTRAT Demonstration
5	Case #1 Discussion
6	Image and Competitive Position; ASTRAT Demonstration
7	Case #2 Discussion PROJECT REPORT (PART 1) DUE: COMMUNICATION OBJECTIVES
	III. *Budgeting and Media Planning*
8	Budgeting; ASTRAT Demonstration
9	Media Selection
10	Media Planning Models; ASTRAT Demonstration
11	Case #3 Discussion PROJECT REPORT (PART 2) DUE: ADVERTISING BUDGET AND MEDIA DECISIONS
	IV. *Creating Advertising Campaigns and Measuring their Effectiveness*
12	Creative Strategy
13	Selecting Creative Tactics; ASTRAT Demonstration
14	Case #4 Discussion
15	Case #5 Discussion
16	Measuring Advertising Effectiveness
17	Case #6 Discussion
	V. *Other Topics*
18	Social/Economic Effects of Advertising
19	GROUP PRESENTATIONS
20	GROUP PRESENTATIONS GROUP PROJECT REPORT DUE: THE BRAND ADVERTISING CAMPAIGN

Exhibit 2.3

ADSTRAT PROJECT DESCRIPTION

The objectives of this project are; first, to provide students with an advertising problem that can be solved through team effort, organization, knowledge, and creativity; second, to encourage students to solve problems in a realistic manner; and third to allow students to demonstrate their understanding and mastery of advertising concepts and techniques.

Students will work as teams on an advertising plan for a brand of Sonite using information and analysis tools provided in ASTRAT. Each team should think of itself as the client's advertising agency who is preparing an annual plan to present to an executive committee. Your recommendations should be supported by a careful and detailed analysis of ASTRAT's industry, panel, consumer, and media databases. At the end of the course, each team will turn in a final report consisting of a well-integrated and carefully documented proposal for what strategies, expenditures, and research are to be followed for that product.

PROJECT CONTENT

The project report should address the following topics:

1. *Situation Analysis:* What is this company's business? Provide background information on the company, competitors, and consumers, discuss past advertising activities, and identify relevant trends. What are the characteristics of the various consumer segments? What are consumers' primary motivations for purchasing products and brands? Discuss your brand's liabilities as well as assets. At the end of this section, list problems and opportunities.

2. *Objectives:* What segments are likely to be most profitable? What explicit action and communication objectives should be set for next year's advertising program? How will your brand be positioned relative to competitors? How will the brand satisfy consumers' purchase motivations?

3. *Budget:* What is the necessary budget to achieve your objectives? Include costs for consumer research and copy testing, ad production, media (time and space), and promotions. Consider the audience's size, media habits, and prior knowledge, the responsiveness of the audience to ad expenditures, competitive activities, and the creative strategy of the ad campaign.

———————————————— **Exhibit 2.3** ————————————————

(*continued*)

4. *Copy Strategy and Creative Program:* What should be the overall creative strategy? This will require an assessment of the competition, judgments as to the important points of appeal or differentiation, and consideration of alternative theories of communication and attitude change. How will advertising communicate the brand's benefits in a compelling or engaging way? In what ways will the ad executions be creative and original? Discuss the rationale behind each sample execution. The project report should also spell out the copy-testing research program that you would recommend, giving attention to budget and alternative types of commercial services. The project is designed to place greater emphasis on the originality, relevance, and feasibility of ideas, rather than the elaborate nature of the report's presentation. Consequently, only rough storyboards for television commercials and semi-comprehensive layouts for print advertising are required. It is not necessary to provide type set for production, photographs, finished artwork, taped radio commercials, or videotaped/filmed television commercials.

5. *Media Strategy and Budget:* Here you are to recommend the overall media mix to be used, showing a breakdown of expenses by alternative media. (This should include money for promotional materials, contests, prizes, etc., where applicable.) Illustrate your media schedule with a calendar of marketing activities. Discuss the rationale behind your media strategy, including reach, frequency, and source effects. Assess the relevance of available media models and research services.

Teams *may not solicit assistance or counsel* from other teams or advertising practitioners. You may consult with media representatives and research suppliers for additional cost information. Any published research materials may be utilized. *Make your own decisions* about appropriate communication objectives, budget, creative strategy, and media planning.

PROJECT REPORT

At the end of the course, each team will submit a typed final report (not to exceed 20 double-spaced pages) complete with specific objectives, detailed budget, media plan, creative rationale and examples, and other sales promotion activity. Unlimited exhibits are allowed, but any exhibits should be relevant and should support the proposed advertising plan. The most important information from exhibits should be discussed in the narrative and sources of exhibit material should be identified. (Printouts from the ASTRAT program can be included as supporting exhibits.) You must show the link between situation analysis, objectives, budgeting, media planning, creative strategy, and ad executions. If you make an assumption, note that it is an assumption.

Projects will be evaluated on the basis of overall communication effectiveness and the degree to which lecture and textbook concepts, models, and techniques are integrated into the presentation.

Here are a few suggestions for the format of the report. Include a table of contents, an introduction, and a conclusion. Provide a budget summary page, a schedule of media activities, and a complete list of references. Use headings and subheadings. Write in prose rather than outline format. Number pages. Do not right-justify (it's harder to read). Check for spelling and typographical errors.

Group projects will receive a single grade. Any problems of unequal contributions by individual group members must be resolved by the group itself. In extreme cases, a group may split up because of the failure of one group member to participate. If this occurs, each individual must (a) submit his or her own report meeting all of the usual requirements, or (b) drop the course, or (c) receive a score of zero on the final project. Successful completion of the project is a major requirement of the course, so you should start on the project as soon as possible.

NO LATE PROJECTS WILL BE ACCEPTED.

3

Introducing ASTRAT to Students

The following pages (in Exhibit 3.1) provide transparency masters which can be used to introduce ADSTRAT to the class and summarize key elements of the ADSTRAT system. The slides review information which is presented in the first two chapters of the student manual:

1. An Introduction to Decision Support Systems
2. ADSTRAT Objectives
3. Principles Guiding the Design of ADSTRAT
4. Description of the ADSTRAT Data Bases
5. Description ofADSTRAT Modules

The slides on the specific options of the ADSTRAT modules can be delayed until the class sessions when the corresponding advertising decisions are discussed.

We also find it helpful to have an introductory class session describing the installation and operation of ADSTRAT. This material is covered in the Appendix of the student manual. The instructor can demonstrate the options on ADSTRAT's main menu, and show students how to load, save, and print module parameters and output.

Exhibit 3.1

Transparencies
for
ADSTRAT Introduction

ADSTRAT

AN ADVERTISING DECISION SUPPORT SYSTEM

Hubert Gatignon
The Wharton School
University of Pennsylvania

Raymond R. Burke
Harvard Business School
Harvard University

WHY A DECISION SUPPORT SYSTEM IN ADVERTISING MANAGEMENT?

- Increasing environmental complexity
- Increasing decision complexity
- Increasing amounts of information
- Qualitative and quantitative considerations
- Learning Tool

DECISION SUPPORT SYSTEM
DEFINITION

An advertising decision support system is a coordinated collection of data, models, analytical tools, and computer power by which an organization gathers information from its environment and turns it into a basis for advertising decisions.

ADSTRAT: An Advertising Decision Support System

OBJECTIVES

ADSTRAT offers an integrated system where different approaches and methodologies can be applied to various types of data.

Different Data
- sales and competitive decision data
- survey data (e.g., psychographics)
- secondary data (e.g., media information)
- managerial judgments
- expert knowledge

Different Approaches
- statistical inference (e.g., regression)
- analytic algorithms (e.g., cluster analysis)
- optimization models (e.g., linear programming)
- simulations (e.g., ADBUDG)
- expert systems

Different Levels of Complexity
   e.g., linear programming versus MEDIAC

ADSTRAT: An Advertising Decision Support System

PRINCIPLES GUIDING
THE DESIGN OF ADSTRAT

- *To emphasize advertising decisions and concepts rather than methodologies*

  - Analysis tools are grouped by advertising decision

  - Data relevant to a particular analysis are automatically accessed

- *To encourage what-if analyses*

  - Keep as much input and output information in view as possible so that the user can consider and modify the various options and observe the results

ADSTRAT DATA

Industry Level Data Base
(by period, by brand)

- Price

- Advertising expenditures

- Product characteristics

- Sales force size by channel

- Unit cost

- Number of distributors by channel

- Sales (in units and in $)

- Market share (based on units and on $)

ADSTRAT: An Advertising Decision Support System

ADSTRAT DATA

Panel Data Base
(by period, by brand, by segment)

- Brand awareness

- Brand perceptions

- Preferences (ideal points and distance from ideal points on each dimension)

- Purchase intent

- Percentage of segment shopping in each channel

- Market segment shares

- Segment sizes (unit sales)

ADSTRAT DATA

Survey Data Base

- Demographics

- Attitudes

- Opinions

- Interests

- Lifestyles

- Product usage

- Decision Process

- Media habits

ADSTRAT DATA

Media Data Base

- Vehicle audience
- Cost per insertion

ADSTRAT: An Advertising Decision Support System

ADSTRAT MODULES

- Situation Analysis

- Communication Objectives

- Budget Decisions

- Copy Design

- Media and Scheduling Decisions

ADSTRAT: An Advertising Decision Support System

SITUATION ANALYSIS MODULE

- Trend Analysis

- Describe Consumers: Psychographics and Factor Analysis

- Classify Consumers: Cluster Analysis

- Profile Consumers: Cross Tabulation

- Profile Consumers: Regression Analysis

COMMUNICATION OBJECTIVES MODULE

- Communication Assessment

- Competitive Positioning

- An Expert System for Communication Objectives

ADVERTISING BUDGET DECISION MODULE

- Advertising to Sales Ratios

- Measuring Advertising Effectiveness

- Budget Aid: A Decision Aid Model

ADVERTISING COPY DESIGN MODULE

- An Expert System for Copy Design

MEDIA AND SCHEDULING DECISIONS MODULE

- Media Efficiency: Cost per Thousand

- Media Allocation: Linear Programming

- Media Aid: A Decision Aid Model

ADSTRAT MODULES

Demonstration of User Interface

4

Situation Analysis,
Profiling Consumers, &
Target Audience Selection

The transparencies which follow in Exhibit 4.1 can be used to introduce the types of analyses to be performed by the students in order to assess the situation and understand the industry in which their brand is marketed. Then, an in-class demonstration of some of the options in the Situation analysis module helps students to get acquainted with ADSTRAT. Examples follow the transparencies for the session.

At the outset, it should be pointed out to the students that a thorough analysis of the situation is critical at the beginning of the advertising planning process because specific advertising decisions require background information which can only be gained through that analysis. The students must therefore consider the various consumer and market factors outlined in the transparencies.

The segmentation problem is best solved by following a five-step procedure outlined in the accompanying transparencies. The transparencies demonstrate a series of analyses leading to five segments corresponding to those described in the manual. If you are using a slower (8086 or 80286) computer to demonstrate how to use the situation analysis module in class, the execution time required to perform the procedures prevents analyzing many variables. If you use a small set of variables (e.g., 10), the in-class demonstration will not provide the most reliable and useful results. It is nevertheless helpful to go quickly through some examples in class to show students how to interact with the software. The demonstration runs included as transparencies in Exhibit 4.1 are small examples which can be run quickly in class for illustration purposes, but which do not lead to the actual segments reported in the manual. These can be used as examples to be shown in class.

Step 1: *Select a subset of statements which reflect various personality and life-style characteristics that might be associated with ownership of the Sonite product or a particular brand of Sonite. Only continuous variables can be selected.*

While it would be possible on a main frame computer to run a factor analysis on all of the variables in the data set, there are two reasons why it should not be attempted with the ADSTRAT system. First, the Personal Computer has the advantage of enabling a user-friendly interface. However, a drawback is that the size of memory available is limited. (At the present time, ADSTRAT uses up to 640 KB of system memory, but does not use expanded or extended memory.) No more than approximately twenty variables can be factor analyzed on a PC with ADSTRAT. Second, from a pedagogical point of view, this first step constitutes an opportunity to force students to think about what they are doing rather than letting the computer automatically do certain types of analyses.

It is recommended that students do not include demographic variables at this point, as the objective is to reduce the number of psychographic statements in order to summarize them with the fewest dimensions possible without losing information.

Step 2: *Reduce the large collection of variables to a smaller set of independent factors (Describe Consumers option).*

When using factor analysis, if students are not familiar with the Factor Analysis technique from a market research or multivariate statistics course, they should be told to consider only the subset of the output showing the rotated factor pattern. These related factors can be interpreted by identifying the statements loading high on each factor and inferring the shared concepts. There should be three factors emanating from the factor analysis, which can be interpreted as: (1) socially active, fashion concious; (2) cultural orientation; and (3) family love, conservative orientation.

Step 3: *Group respondents into homogeneous clusters based on the similarity of their factor scores and demographics (Classify Consumers option).*

Respondents could be clustered into groups using the original psychographic statements. However, it is easier to interpret the results if one uses the factor scores obtained from the factor analysis. Demographic characteristics should be included in this analysis to complement the psychographic characteristics summarized by the factor scores. Although media habits could be included at this stage in the analysis, it is preferable to identify the clusters first, and then look at the relationship between cluster membership and media habits. Purchase decision process variables could also be included among the variables checked. The user might then interpret the clusters by comparing the variable means across clusters, instead of performing a separate analysis using cross-tabulations, as illustrated below.

Students who are not familiar with statistical techniques from a marketing research course should not be concerned with the dendrogram, which indicates the relative similarity of the clusters. Instead, they should examine the cluster centroids, which are the mean values of the variables included in the cluster analysis for each cluster.

Step 4: *Cross-tabulate cluster membership with categorical variables (such as income, socio-professional characteristics, etc.) or continuous variables (such as purchase decision process variables).*

Cross-tabs are used to see how the groups differ in terms of a number of characteristics which were not part of the cluster analysis. These variables include categorical variables such as marital status, household income, occupation or geographical location. The means of the variables included in the cluster analysis are shown for each group in the output of cluster analysis. Regression results can also be used to provide information about the relationship between the factors and the dependent (continuous) variable of your choice. These relationships are useful to interpret the clusters. In particular, when "cluster" is selected as the independent variable, dummy variables are created for each cluster, and the regression results indicate how the mean of the dependent variable differs across clusters (relative to the last cluster, which corresponds to the intercept).

Step 5: *Interpret the meaning of the segments.*

Segment numbers do not correspond to cluster numbers. The segmentation provided in the panel data set is primarily based on demographics and easily accessible household variables. When analyzing personality and life style characteristics, a different segmentation scheme could result. However, because demographic variables (e.g., age) are often associated with lifestyle traits (e.g., cultural interests), there should be a relatively good match between the interpretation of the clusters and the segments. The five segments are described in Chapter 2 of the ADSTRAT manual. Segment 1 consists primarily of the "buffs," or experts in the product category. They are innovators and have high standards and requirements in terms of technical quality of the product. Segment 2 is composed of "singles" who are relatively knowledgeable about the product but somewhat price sensitive. "Professionals" are found mostly in Segment 3. They are demanding in terms of product quality and are willing to pay a premium price for that quality. "High earners" constitute Segment 4. These individuals are also relatively price insensitive. However, they are not as educated as the professionals, and are not particularly knowledgeable about the product category. They buy the product mostly to enhance their social status. The fifth and last segment covers all consumers who cannot be grouped with any of the other four segments. They have used the product less than consumers in other segments and are considered to be late adopters of this product category. Given that this group is identified as a residual, it is more difficult to characterize the members in terms of demographics or lifestyle.

EXAMPLES OF SEGMENTATION ANALYSES

The following analyses provide a description of the process for deriving consumer segments which correspond to the segments described in the manual.

First, the user selects a set of variables for factor analysis which reflect an intuitive assessment of possible a priori dimensions. Five possible groups of variables are listed below, representing 21 of the original survey items.

1st Dimension—Family orientation

ClothesFresh
WashHands
TooMuchSex
Mother
CloseFamily

2nd Dimension—Fashion orientation

TryHairdo
LatStyl
DressSmart
BrightFun

3rd Dimension—Social orientation

Sportng
Social
Exercis
Parties

4th Dimension—Food orientation

GrocShp
LikeBaking
SaveRecipes
LikeKitchen

5th Dimension—Cultural orientation

LikeMaid
ServDinners
ClassicMusic
TripWorld

The factor analysis which follows in Exhibit 4.2 results in three factors. These factors can be interpreted as follows:

Factor 1: Dynamism/Social interaction.

Factor 2: Traditional/no interest in cultural things.

Factor 3: Fashion consciousness.

Next, the user clusters respondents into groups using the factor scores (to summarize the psychographic dimensions) as well as additional demographic variables (see Exhibit 4.3). Five clusters are identified. These five clusters correspond to the following segments:

Cluster 1 = Segment 2

Cluster 2 = Segment 1

Cluster 3 = Segment 5

Cluster 4 = Segment 4

Cluster 5 = Segment 3

The relationship between the clusters and the segments can be identified by comparing the centroid values across clusters, and by cross-tabulating the "cluster" variable with other variables not included in the cluster analysis. For example, Cluster 1 has the lowest score on age and on household size. This characterizes the single segment. Cross-tabulation by occupation (Exhibit 4.4) indicates that Clusters 4 and 5 are individuals who are professionals, managers, or administrators. In addition, while individuals in Cluster 5 are knowledgeable about Sonites, those in Cluster 4 are not (as indicated by cross-tabulating the "cluster" variable with knowledge about Sonites, as shown in Exhibit 4.5). Therefore, Cluster 5 corresponds to the Professionals while Cluster 4, which groups older individuals, corresponds to the high earners. This can be also confirmed by a cross-tab with income, which shows that the income of households in Clusters 4 and 5 is at least $50,000, but less than that for the other segments. It is possible to discriminate between the two remaining clusters (2 and 3) on the basis of their difference in knowledge about Sonites. Cluster 2 shows a high knowledge about Sonites while Cluster 3 has a low knowledge. Therefore, Cluster 2 is the buffs segment and Cluster 3 corresponds to the others (Segment 5).

Once the segments have been identified, it is now possible to derive a much more complete profile of each segment than what is provided in the manual. Psychographic variables, purchase behavior, and media vehicle readership and viewership information are all available in the survey dataset. This information will be particularly useful for designing advertising copy and selecting media vehicles.

Exhibit 4.1

Transparencies for
Situation Analysis,
Profiling Consumers, and
Target Audience Selection

SITUATION ANALYSIS, PROFILING CONSUMERS AND TARGET AUDIENCE SELECTION

- Product Analysis

- Market Analysis

- Consumer Analysis

PRODUCT ANALYSIS

- Analysis of the physical product

- Analysis of the product image

- Analysis of the importance of attributes

- Analysis of advertising

MARKET ANALYSIS

- Market structure

- Segmentation of market

- Market forecasts

- Social, cultural and legal trends

CONSUMER ANALYSIS

- Product and brand purchase motivation

- Decision making unit

- Decision process

- Consumer behavior

- Consumer characteristics

- Communication Channels

SEGMENTATION ANALYSIS:
PROFILING CONSUMERS

Step 1: Select a subset of statements which reflect various personality and life-style characteristics that might be associated with ownership of the Sonite product or a particular brand of Sonite. Only continuous variables can be selected.

Step 2: Reduce the collection of variables to a smaller set of independent factors (Describe Consumers option).

Step 3: Group respondents into homogeneous clusters based on the similarity of their factor scores and demographics (Classify Consumers option).

Step 4: Cross-tabulate cluster membership with categorical variables (such as Income, Socio-professional characteristics, etc.) or continuous variables (such as purchase decision process variables).

Step 5: Interpret the meaning of the segments.

SITUATION ANALYSIS, PROFILING CONSUMERS AND TARGET AUDIENCE SELECTION

Demonstration Runs

ADSTRAT: An Advertising Decision Support System

Output from Module:Situation:Describe
Dataset: survey.dat

ADSTRAT Version 1.0
Copyright 1991, 1992

Parameter file:
Fri Apr 10 13:17:07 1992

H. Gatignon & R. Burke

DESCRIBE CONSUMERS--PSYCHOGRAPHICS AND FACTOR ANALYSIS

Initial Factor Pattern

	Factor 1	Factor 2	Factor 3
TryHairdo	0.534	-0.555	0.449
DressSmart	0.517	-0.570	0.448
ClothesFresh	-0.899	0.155	0.080
FeelAttract	0.720	-0.181	-0.548
Social	0.716	-0.141	-0.573
LikeMaid	0.492	0.750	0.139
ServDinners	0.452	0.778	-.129
SaveRecipes	-0.841	-0.270	-0.201
LikeKitchen	-0.837	-0.232	-0.185
Children	-0.891	0.202	0.053

Number of significant factors: 3

Variance Explained by Each Unrotated Factor

	Variance Explained	Cumulative Variance	Percentage Explained	Cumulative Percentage
Factor 1	5.039	5.039	62.7	62.7
Factor 2	2.043	7.082	25.4	88.1
Factor 3	1.151	8.232	14.3	102.4
Factor 4	0.198	8.430	2.5	104.8
Factor 5	-0.027	8.403	-0.3	104.5
Factor 6	-0.041	8.362	-0.5	104.0
Factor 7	-0.064	8.298	-0.8	103.2
Factor 8	-0.078	8.220	-1.0	102.2
Factor 9	-0.087	8.133	-1.1	101.1
Factor 10	-0.092	8.041	-1.1	100.0

ADSTRAT: An Advertising Decision Support System

Rotated Factor Pattern

	Factor 1	Factor 2	Factor 3
TryHairdo	-0.152	-0.018	0.878
DressSmart	-0.145	-0.039	0.878
ClothesFresh	0.694	-0.343	-0.490
FeelAttract	-0.911	0.090	0.115
Social	-0.918	0.113	0.074
LikeMaid	-0.079	0.898	-0.098
ServDinners	-0.055	0.896	-0.141
SaveRecipes	0.368	-0.727	-0.395
LikeKitchen	0.384	-0.690	-0.405
Children	0.678	-0.309	-0.531

Variance Explained By Each Rotated Factor

	Variance Explained	Cumulative Variance	Percentage Explained	Cumulative Percentage
Factor 1	2.948	2.948	35.8	35.8
Factor 2	2.851	5.800	34.6	70.4
Factor 3	2.433	8.232	29.6	100.0

ADSTRAT: An Advertising Decision Support System

Output from Module:Situation:Classify
Dataset: survey.dat,factor.dat

ADSTRAT Version 1.0
Copyright 1991, 1992

Parameter file:
Tue Jul 21 16:14:28 1992

H. Gatignon & R. Burke

CLASSIFY CONSUMERS — CLUSTER ANALYSIS

Cluster #	1	2	3	4	5
Observations	82	48	47	64	59
Centroids					
Age	22.122	39.229	39.660	41.875	47.763
HHSize	1.195	1.813	5.383	2.406	5.305
Factor01	-0.647	0.975	0.934	-0.205	0.185
Factor02	0.176	-0.281	-0.236	0.926	0.812
Factor03	0.471	-0.695	-0.698	-0.721	-0.997

Dendrogram

```
* * * * * * * * * * * * * * * * *    Tvalue   df
* *      * * * * * * * * * * * * *   35.138   298
* *      * * * * *      * * * * *    37.176   216
* *      * *    * *     * * * * * *  17.870   93
* *      * *    * *    * *    * *     16.902   121
 1       2      3      4     5
```

ADSTRAT: An Advertising Decision Support System

Output from Module:Situation:Tabulate   ADSTRAT Version 1.0
Dataset: survey.dat,factor.dat,cluster.dat   Copyright 1991, 1992

Fri Apr 10 13:20:14 1992   H. Gatignon & R. Burke

CROSS TABULATION

Cluster		Education 1	2	3	4	5	6	7
1	Freq	0	0	24	21	30	7	0
	Perct	0.00	0.00	8.00	7.00	10.00	2.33	0.00
	Row %	0.00	0.00	29.27	25.61	36.59	8.54	0.00
	Col %	0.00	0.00	58.54	17.36	47.62	15.22	0.00
2	Freq	3	3	11	31	0	0	0
	Perct	1.00	1.00	3.67	10.33	0.00	0.00	0.00
	Row %	6.25	6.25	22.92	64.58	0.00	0.00	0.00
	Col %	60.00	75.00	26.83	25.62	0.00	0.00	0.00
3	Freq	2	1	6	37	1	0	0
	Perct	0.67	0.33	2.00	12.33	0.33	0.00	0.00
	Row %	4.26	2.13	12.77	78.72	2.13	0.00	0.00
	Col %	40.00	25.00	14.63	30.58	1.59	0.00	0.00
4	Freq	0	0	0	8	13	29	14
	Perct	0.00	0.00	0.00	2.67	4.33	9.67	4.67
	Row %	0.00	0.00	0.00	12.50	20.31	45.31	21.88
	Col %	0.00	0.00	0.00	6.61	20.63	63.04	70.00
5	Freq	0	0	0	24	19	10	6
	Perct	0.00	0.00	0.00	8.00	6.33	3.33	2.00
	Row %	0.00	0.00	0.00	40.68	32.20	16.95	10.17
	Col %	0.00	0.00	0.00	19.83	30.16	21.74	30.00

Chi Square   = 219.154
Degree of freedom = 24

Exhibit 4.2

Output from Module:Situation:Describe   ADSTRAT Version 1.0
Dataset: survey.dat   Copyright 1991, 1992

Parameter file: H. Gatignon & R. Burke
Mon Apr 06 18:06:31 1992

DESCRIBE CONSUMERS--PSYCHOGRAPHICS
AND FACTOR ANALYSIS

Initial Factor Pattern

	Factor 1	Factor 2	Factor 3
TryHairdo	0.556	0.571	-0.437
LatStyl	0.567	0.587	-0.432
DressSmart	0.541	0.588	-0.449
GrocShp	-0.819	0.302	0.220
LikeBaking	-0.838	0.279	0.166
ClothesFresh	-0.915	-0.133	-0.089
WashHands	-0.919	-0.134	-0.061
Sportng	0.720	0.150	0.571
TooMuchSex	-0.912	-0.167	-0.051
Social	0.722	0.083	0.581
LikeMaid	0.474	-0.759	-0.193
ServDinners	0.425	-0.793	-0.183
SaveRecipes	-0.833	0.296	0.214
LikeKitchen	-0.833	0.265	0.199
Mother	-0.906	-0.175	-0.023
ClassicMusic	0.430	-0.803	-0.144
CloseFamily	-0.910	-0.183	-0.027
Exercis	0.734	0.133	0.580
TripWorld	0.470	-0.779	-0.126
Parties	0.725	0.127	0.583
BrightFun	0.485	0.633	-0.459

Number of significant factors: 3

Variance Explained by Each Unrotated Factor

	Variance Explained	Cumulative Variance	Percentage Explained	Cumulative Percentage
Factor 1	10.998	10.998	61.1	61.1
Factor 2	4.393	15.391	24.4	85.5
Factor 3	2.415	17.805	13.4	98.9
Factor 4	0.516	18.321	2.9	101.8
Factor 5	0.041	18.362	0.2	102.0
Factor 6	0.024	18.386	0.1	102.2
Factor 7	0.016	18.402	0.1	102.2
Factor 8	0.012	18.415	0.1	102.3
Factor 9	0.000	18.415	0.0	102.3
Factor10	-0.008	18.407	-0.0	102.3
Factor11	-0.009	18.398	-0.0	102.2
Factor12	-0.017	18.381	-0.1	102.1
Factor13	-0.026	18.355	-0.1	102.0
Factor14	-0.029	18.326	-0.2	101.8
Factor15	-0.033	18.293	-0.2	101.6
Factor16	-0.036	18.257	-0.2	101.4
Factor17	-0.042	18.215	-0.2	101.2
Factor18	-0.047	18.167	-0.3	100.9
Factor19	-0.051	18.116	-0.3	100.7
Factor20	-0.057	18.059	-0.3	100.3
Factor21	-0.061	17.998	-0.3	100.0

Rotated Factor Pattern

	Factor 1	Factor 2	Factor 3
TryHairdo	0.161	0.017	0.895
LatStyl	0.174	0.025	0.907
DressSmart	0.144	0.035	0.905
GrocShp	-0.353	0.738	-0.375
LikeBaking	-0.408	0.713	-0.364
ClothesFresh	-0.710	0.346	-0.489
WashHands	-0.692	0.356	-0.510
Sportng	0.922	-0.075	0.100
TooMuchSex	-0.686	0.331	-0.532
Social	0.921	-0.126	0.055
LikeMaid	0.063	-0.909	-0.089
ServDinners	0.031	-0.907	-0.140
SaveRecipes	-0.368	0.740	-0.382
LikeKitchen	-0.383	0.710	-0.391
Mother	-0.663	0.330	-0.551
ClassicMusic	0.060	-0.905	-0.169
CloseFamily	-0.670	0.325	-0.555
Exercis	0.936	-0.093	0.092
TripWorld	0.104	-0.901	-0.145
Parties	0.931	-0.092	0.081
BrightFun	0.106	0.096	0.909

Variance Explained By Each Rotated Factor

	Variance Explained	Cumulative Variance	Percentage Explained	Cumulative Percentage
Factor 1	6.464	6.464	36.3	36.3
Factor 2	6.004	12.468	33.7	70.0
Factor 3	5.338	17.805	30.0	100.0

Exhibit 4.3

Output from Module:Situation:Classify   ADSTRAT Version 1.0
Dataset: survey.dat,factor.dat   Copyright 1991, 1992

Parameter file: H. Gatignon & R. Burke
Tue Jul 21 15:42:25 1992

CLASSIFY CONSUMERS — CLUSTER ANALYSIS

Cluster #	1	2	3	4	5
Observations	65	33	96	53	53
Centroids					
Age	24.077	24.727	39.813	50.208	41.415
HHSize	1.031	1.879	3.531	4.000	4.245
Factor01	0.752	-0.568	-0.167	0.281	1.071
Factor02	0.034	-0.573	1.048	0.122	-0.246
Factor03	-0.786	1.141	-0.881	-0.403	-0.825

Dendrogram

```
* * * * * * * * * * * * * * * * *     Tvalue   df
* * * * * *     * * * * * * * * *     24.526  298
* *     * *     * * * * * * * * *     50.593   96
* *     * *     * *     * * * * * *   32.897  200
* *     * *     * *     * *     * *   22.571  104
 1       2       3       4       5
```

52

Output from Module:Situation:Tabulate   ADSTRAT Version 1.0
Dataset: survey.dat,factor.dat,cluster.dat   Copyright 1991, 1992

Tue Apr 07 10:38:53 1992   H. Gatignon & R. Burke

CROSS TABULATION

		Occupation					
Cluster		0	1	2	3	4	9
1	Freq	0	6	5	26	28	0
	Perct	0.00	2.00	1.67	8.67	9.33	0.00
	Row %	0.00	9.23	7.69	40.00	43.08	0.00
	Col %	0.00	12.24	6.10	34.21	82.35	0.00
2	Freq	0	12	0	15	6	0
	Perct	0.00	4.00	0.00	5.00	2.00	0.00
	Row %	0.00	36.36	0.00	45.45	18.18	0.00
	Col %	0.00	24.49	0.00	19.74	17.65	0.00
3	Freq	2	0	2	35	0	57
	Perct	0.67	0.00	0.67	11.67	0.00	19.00
	Row %	2.08	0.00	2.08	36.46	0.00	59.38
	Col %	100.00	0.00	2.44	46.05	0.00	100.00
4	Freq	0	0	53	0	0	0
	Perct	0.00	0.00	17.67	0.00	0.00	0.00
	Row %	0.00	0.00	100.00	0.00	0.00	0.00
	Col %	0.00	0.00	64.63	0.00	0.00	0.00
5	Freq	0	31	22	0	0	0
	Perct	0.00	10.33	7.33	0.00	0.00	0.00
	Row %	0.00	58.49	41.51	0.00	0.00	0.00
	Col %	0.00	63.27	26.83	0.00	0.00	0.00

Chi Square   = 488.754
Degree of freedom = 20

Exhibit 4.5

Output from Module:Situation:Tabulate   ADSTRAT Version 1.0
Dataset: survey.dat,factor.dat,cluster.dat   Copyright 1991, 1992

Tue Apr 07 10:39:47 1992   H. Gatignon & R. Burke

CROSS TABULATION

		KnowledgeSon	
Cluster		2 - 5	6 - 7
	Freq	4	61
1	Perct	1.33	20.33
	Row %	6.15	93.85
	Col %	2.58	42.07
	Freq	0	33
2	Perct	0.00	11.00
	Row %	0.00	100.00
	Col %	0.00	22.76
	Freq	96	0
3	Perct	32.00	0.00
	Row %	100.00	0.00
	Col %	61.94	0.00
	Freq	53	0
4	Perct	17.67	0.00
	Row %	100.00	0.00
	Col %	34.19	0.00
	Freq	2	51
5	Perct	0.67	17.00
	Row %	3.77	96.23
	Col %	1.29	35.17

Chi Square   = 277.261
Degree of freedom = 4

5

Objectives

The class discussion of communication objectives is divided into three parts: (1) a discussion of the reasons for setting objectives, (2) the elaboration of a list of possible marketing and advertising objectives, and (3) the evaluation of objectives. The transparencies at the end of this chapter (Exhibit 5.1) provide the outline for these class discussions. The transparency on the hierarchy-of-effects can be left blank by the instructor so that he or she can elicit the hierarchy from the students and write it in during the discussion.

The ADSTRAT advertising planning project presupposes that, at this stage, the students know which brand they will be advertising. There are two options for the instructor. The instructor can either assign specific brands to the groups of students, or, alternatively, assign firms to groups and allow the students to pick which brand to advertise from among the brands marketed by the firm in Period 8. The advantages of the first option are that (1) the instructor can manage the variety of brands that he or she desires, and (2) students can start working right away on the objectives. If the instructor lets the students choose the specific brand, the students must develop criteria for their choice and understand the industry they are in. This option has the advantage of forcing students to do a thorough situation analysis of the industry.

Let's assume that a group has been assigned Firm O, which markets the brands SOLD and SONO. The first preliminary step to the selection of objectives is to choose a brand. It helps the students to give them examples of criteria to use to select their brand. For example: are you interested in managing a brand which has a low or a high market share? Do you prefer to sell to a market which is growing or which is at the maturity stage of its life cycle? Do you like to work with a brand which has recently been introduced or a brand which has been on the market for a few years? Once they have developed a set of criteria, students can then use trend analysis to identify which segments are growing, the share of each of the brands, etc. For example, the trend analysis of variable SegSize indicates the growth of each segment, as illustrated in the output presented in Exhibits 5.2–5.6. These output are obtained by selecting one segment and one brand. The reason for selecting a single brand is that the value of SegSize is the same for all the brands. If more than one brand is selected, the plot can become over-crowded. The plots clearly indicate that Segments 2, 4 and 5 are growing, although Segment 5 seems to be following an S-shaped diffusion with a possible sign of saturation. Segments 1 and 3 seem to be at the maturity stage of the product life cycle.

Next, it is necessary to find out about the market structure in terms of the market share of each brand in each market. This can be obtained by performing a trend analysis on market share for each brand and segment. However, it is more efficient to use the CommAssess option of the Objectives module. The output for Period 8 is shown in Exhibit 5.7. If interested in a growing segment such as the singles (Segment 2), it can be seen that brand SONO has the highest share (43.8%), followed by brand SULU (30.8%), and SARK (10.2%). These three brands appear to be the three largest competitors in this segment. On the basis of this information, brand SONO can be chosen.

Once a brand has been chosen, the research data on the hierarchy of effect measures can help the user to identify possible communication problems. Indeed, looking at the Communication Assessment output for Segment 2 in Period 8, it appears that SONO may have a problem with preferences. All three brands competing seriously in this segment have a relatively high awareness, with SONO leading the group. Nevertheless, the purchase intentions of SONO are lower than those of SULU. The fact that SULU's share is lower might indicate a distribution or production problem with SULU. However, the weak performance of SONO at the purchase intention level of the hierarchy of effects suggests that consumers may have relatively poor perceptions of this brand. While consumers' perceptions of SONO on the first and third dimensions are the same as SULU, on Dimension 2, SONO has a 5.71 and SULU has a 5.10. It seems that communication could be directed at maintaining the awareness level of SONO above the level of the competitors and/or that perceptions on Dimension 2 (perception of power) should be modified.

The Positioning option shown in Exhibit 5.8 confirms that the three brands competing for Segment 2 are SONO, SULU, and SARK, and that SONO is perceived as having too much power relative to this segment's preferences. It should be noted that the perceptual map presents better information than ComAssess for identifying the brand's competitors. This is because a brand could have a low share as indicated in the Communication Assessment output due to low awareness (if the brand is just being introduced) but still be a serious competitive threat because of its positioning.

In summary, the objectives of SONO should be to reposition the brand closer to the ideal brand for that segment. The distance from its current position to the objective perceptions is not so large that a change in the physical product is needed. It is likely that the persuasive power of advertising can reposition the brand. Another objective to consider is to maintain or increase the top-of-mind awareness of the brand. The Advisor option can be used to confirm and refine these objectives. The questions asked during the session can be answered using information obtained from the trend analyses and by cross-tabulating cluster membership with purchase decision process questions. Exhibit 5.9 presents an example consultation with Advisor, and lists the sources for each of the user inputs.

Exhibit 5.1

Transparencies
for
Advertising Objectives

ADVERTISING OBJECTIVES

- Why do you need objectives?

- Objectives:

    ◦ What variable(s)?

    ◦ What level?

BENEFITS OF OBJECTIVES

- Direction

- Coordination

- Decision Criteria

- Feedback

DAGMAR:
Defining Advertising Goals for
Measured Advertising Results

- An approach to advertising planning.

- A method for selecting and quantifying goals.

- A method for measuring communication effects.

HIERARCHY OF EFFECTS

Awareness

Image

Attitude

Preference

Purchase (Trial)

Repeat Purchase (Loyalty)

Satisfaction

ADSTRAT: An Advertising Decision Support System

ADVERTISING GOALS
Definition

1   Communication goals,

2   expressed in written, finite, measurable terms,

3   agreed upon,

4   based on research, and

5   tied to benchmarks.

MARKETING OBJECTIVES

An increase in sales can come from four sources:

1.   New customers

    - Nonusers
    - Competitor-loyals

2.   Increased loyalty of existing customers

    - Increase switching in
    - Reduce switching out

3.   Increased usage of existing customers

    - Purchase drives consumption
    - Create new uses

4.   Old customers

    - Attract trier-rejectors

COMMUNICATION OBJECTIVES

Before purchasing a brand, the consumer must:

1. Have a salient need,

2. Be aware of a brand that can satisfy this need,

3. Be able to identify the brand and discriminate between brands at the time of choice, and

4. Have no barriers to purchase.

Advertising can:

1. Stimulate category need,

2. Create brand awareness, facilitate brand recognition and recall,

3. Create brand attitude,

4. Reduce or remove purchase obstacles

ADVERTISING OBJECTIVES

1. Attention

2. Recall (unaided, aided)

    - Advertising recall
    - Brand recall

3. Perception

4. Attitude

5. Preference

6. Behavior intentions

7. Behavior

    - Inquiries
    - Individual choice
    - Aggregate sales

WHY USE INTERMEDIARY VARIABLES, RATHER THAN SALES?

Hierarchy	Decision Relevance	Ease of Measuring
Awareness	Lo	Hi
Image		
	↓	↑
Attitude		
Sales	Hi	Lo

CRITERIA FOR GOOD OBJECTIVES

- Defined audience (target)

- Measurable

- Starting point

- Fixed time period

- Written

Exhibit 5.2

Output from Module:Situation:Trends   ADSTRAT Version 1.0
Dataset: indup.dat,panel.dat   Copyright 1991, 1992
Tue July 21 16:20:16 1992   H. Gatignon & R. Burke

TREND ANALYSIS

Period range 1 to 8
Vertical Axis Variable:SegSize
Horizontal Axis Variable:Period

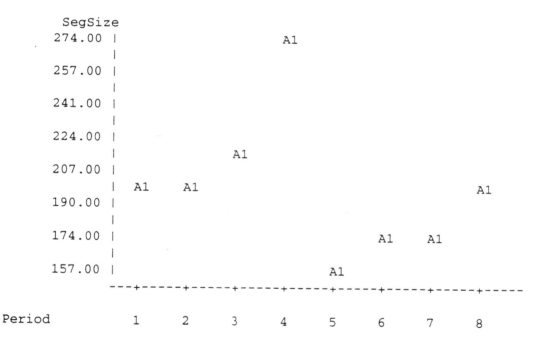

```
     SegSize
    274.00 |                        A1
           |
    257.00 |
           |
    241.00 |
           |
    224.00 |
           |              A1
    207.00 |
           | A1     A1                                      A1
    190.00 |
           |
    174.00 |                             A1    A1
           |
    157.00 |
           ---+-----+-----+-----+-----+-----+-----+-----+-----
                                A1

Period      1     2     3     4     5     6     7     8
```

LEGEND

    Label   Brand(Segment)
    A1   SAMA(1)

Exhibit 5.3

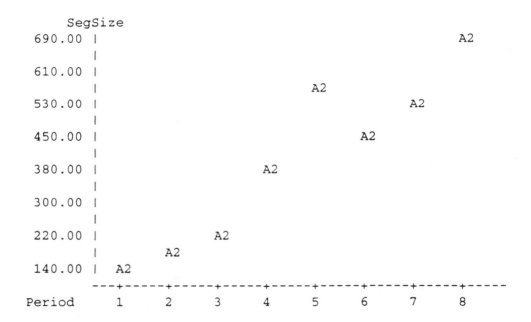

```
Output from Module:Situation:Trends          ADSTRAT Version 1.0
Dataset: indup.dat,panel.dat                 Copyright 1991, 1992
Fri Apr 10 13:53:18 1992                     H. Gatignon & R. Burke
```

TREND ANALYSIS

```
Period range 1 to 8
Vertical Axis Variable:SegSize
Horizontal Axis Variable:Period


       SegSize
   690.00 |                                                   A2
          |
   610.00 |
          |                                 A2
   530.00 |                                            A2
          |
   450.00 |                                      A2
          |
   380.00 |                       A2
          |
   300.00 |
          |
   220.00 |                 A2
          |           A2
   140.00 |   A2
          ---+-----+-----+-----+-----+-----+-----+-----+-----+-----
  Period     1     2     3     4     5     6     7     8
```

LEGEND:

```
   Label          Brand(Segment)
   A2                SAMA(2)
```

Exhibit 5.4

Output from Module:Situation:Trends
Dataset: indup.dat,panel.dat
Fri Apr 10 13:53:48 1992

ADSTRAT Version 1.0
Copyright 1991, 1992
H. Gatignon & R. Burke

TREND ANALYSIS

Period range 1 to 8
Vertical Axis Variable:SegSize
Horizontal Axis Variable:Period

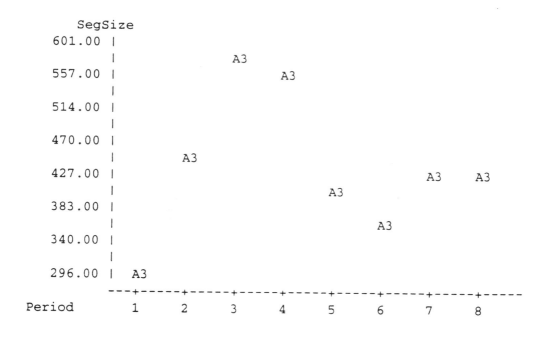

```
    SegSize
   601.00 |
          |                    A3
   557.00 |                         A3
          |
   514.00 |
          |
   470.00 |
          |         A3
   427.00 |                              A3    A3
          |                   A3
   383.00 |
          |                    A3
   340.00 |
          |
   296.00 |  A3
          ---+-----+-----+-----+-----+-----+-----+-----+-----
Period       1     2     3     4     5     6     7     8
```

LEGEND

Label   Brand(Segment)
A3   SAMA(3)

71

Exhibit 5.5

Output from Module:Situation:Trends
Dataset: indup.dat,panel.dat
Fri Apr 10 13:54:27 1992

ADSTRAT Version 1.0
Copyright 1991, 1992
H. Gatignon & R. Burke

TREND ANALYSIS

Period range 1 to 8
Vertical Axis Variable:SegSize
Horizontal Axis Variable:Period

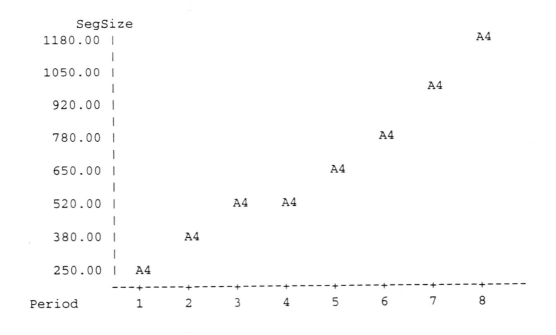

```
     SegSize
 1180.00 |                                          A4
         |
 1050.00 |
         |                                    A4
  920.00 |
         |
  780.00 |                              A4
         |
  650.00 |                        A4
         |
  520.00 |            A4    A4
         |
  380.00 |      A4
         |
  250.00 |  A4
         ---+-----+-----+-----+-----+-----+-----+-----+-----
 Period     1     2     3     4     5     6     7     8
```

LEGEND

Label	Brand(Segment)
A4	SAMA(4)

Exhibit 5.6

```
Output from Module:Situation:Trends          ADSTRAT Version 1.0
Dataset: indup.dat,panel.dat                  Copyright 1991, 1992
Fri Apr 10 13:55:05 1992                      H. Gatignon & R. Burke
```

TREND ANALYSIS

```
Period range 1 to 8
Vertical Axis Variable:SegSize
Horizontal Axis Variable:Period
```

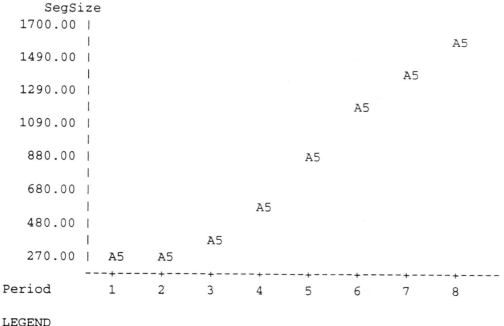

```
       SegSize
  1700.00 |
          |                                                    A5
  1490.00 |
          |                                            A5
  1290.00 |
          |                                    A5
  1090.00 |
          |
   880.00 |                            A5
          |
   680.00 |
          |                    A5
   480.00 |
          |            A5
   270.00 |    A5      A5
          ---+-----+-----+-----+-----+-----+-----+-----+-----
Period       1     2     3     4     5     6     7     8

LEGEND

   Label           Brand(Segment)
    A5                SAMA(5)
```

Output from Module:Objectives:ComAssess   ADSTRAT Version 1.0
Dataset: panel.dat   Copyright 1991, 1992
Fri Apr 10 13:58:36 1992   H. Gatignon & R. Burke

COMMUNICATION ASSESSMENT

Period 8
Segment 1

Brand	Awareness	Perc01	Perc02	Perc03	Intent	Share
SAMA	0.515	2.35	3.03	6.26	0.017	0.014
SALT	0.657	5.49	3.25	6.30	0.042	0.030
SANE	0.487	6.31	5.77	6.45	0.070	0.055
SARK	0.450	3.20	5.61	6.37	0.064	0.052
SEMI	0.697	6.24	5.77	5.70	0.073	0.101
SIBI	0.798	5.35	3.96	5.82	0.098	0.127
SIAA	0.833	1.82	3.34	5.75	0.026	0.031
SOLD	0.652	5.54	5.55	5.73	0.331	0.415
SONO	0.699	2.80	5.71	5.12	0.078	0.072
SULI	0.605	6.17	5.55	5.21	0.120	0.058
SUSI	0.607	2.28	2.91	5.12	0.020	0.013
SULU	0.615	2.80	5.10	5.14	0.061	0.030

Period 8
Segment 2

Brand	Awareness	Perc01	Perc02	Perc03	Intent	Share
SAMA	0.515	2.35	3.03	6.26	0.016	0.018
SALT	0.657	5.49	3.25	6.30	0.007	0.007
SANE	0.487	6.31	5.77	6.45	0.005	0.005
SARK	0.450	3.20	5.61	6.37	0.093	0.102
SEMI	0.697	6.24	5.77	5.70	0.005	0.010
SIBI	0.798	5.35	3.96	5.82	0.012	0.021
SIAA	0.833	1.82	3.34	5.75	0.032	0.053
SOLD	0.652	5.54	5.55	5.73	0.010	0.017
SONO	0.699	2.80	5.71	5.12	0.351	0.438
SULI	0.605	6.17	5.55	5.21	0.006	0.004
SUSI	0.607	2.28	2.91	5.12	0.018	0.017
SULU	0.615	2.80	5.10	5.14	0.444	0.308

Period 8
Segment 3

Brand	Awareness	Perc01	Perc02	Perc03	Intent	Share
SAMA	0.515	2.35	3.03	6.26	0.002	0.002
SALT	0.657	5.49	3.25	6.30	0.010	0.007
SANE	0.487	6.31	5.77	6.45	0.089	0.073
SARK	0.450	3.20	5.61	6.37	0.004	0.004
SEMI	0.697	6.24	5.77	5.70	0.553	0.706
SIBI	0.798	5.35	3.96	5.82	0.020	0.023
SIAA	0.833	1.82	3.34	5.75	0.003	0.004
SOLD	0.652	5.54	5.55	5.73	0.062	0.070
SONO	0.699	2.80	5.71	5.12	0.006	0.005
SULI	0.605	6.17	5.55	5.21	0.243	0.103
SUSI	0.607	2.28	2.91	5.12	0.003	0.002
SULU	0.615	2.80	5.10	5.14	0.005	0.002

Period 8
Segment 4

Brand	Awareness	Perc01	Perc02	Perc03	Intent	Share
SAMA	0.515	2.35	3.03	6.26	0.008	0.006
SALT	0.657	5.49	3.25	6.30	0.129	0.085
SANE	0.487	6.31	5.77	6.45	0.012	0.009
SARK	0.450	3.20	5.61	6.37	0.008	0.006
SEMI	0.697	6.24	5.77	5.70	0.015	0.018
SIBI	0.798	5.35	3.96	5.82	0.739	0.809
SIAA	0.833	1.82	3.34	5.75	0.010	0.010
SOLD	0.652	5.54	5.55	5.73	0.029	0.031
SONO	0.699	2.80	5.71	5.12	0.010	0.008
SULI	0.605	6.17	5.55	5.21	0.020	0.008
SUSI	0.607	2.28	2.91	5.12	0.009	0.005
SULU	0.615	2.80	5.10	5.14	0.011	0.005

Period 8
Segment 5

Brand	Awareness	Perc01	Perc02	Perc03	Intent	Share
SAMA	0.515	2.35	3.03	6.26	0.066	0.064
SALT	0.657	5.49	3.25	6.30	0.005	0.004
SANE	0.487	6.31	5.77	6.45	0.002	0.002
SARK	0.450	3.20	5.61	6.37	0.008	0.008
SEMI	0.697	6.24	5.77	5.70	0.002	0.003
SIBI	0.798	5.35	3.96	5.82	0.006	0.008
SIAA	0.833	1.82	3.34	5.75	0.735	0.817
SOLD	0.652	5.54	5.55	5.73	0.004	0.004
SONO	0.699	2.80	5.71	5.12	0.015	0.012
SULI	0.605	6.17	5.55	5.21	0.003	0.001
SUSI	0.607	2.28	2.91	5.12	0.131	0.067
SULU	0.615	2.80	5.10	5.14	0.023	0.009

```
Output from Module:Objectives:Positioning      ADSTRAT Version 1.0
Dataset: panel.dat                             Copyright 1991, 1992
Fri Apr 10 13:59:28 1992                       H. Gatignon & R. Burke
```

COMPETITIVE POSITIONING
Graph 1

```
Period 8
Vertical Axis Variable:Perc01
Horizontal Axis Variable:Perc02


   Perc01
 7.00 |
      |
 6.10 |                                              a   b3
      |
 5.30 |                    c         d               e
      |                       4
 4.40 |          Hx                                    1
      |
 3.60 |
      |                                          f
 2.70 |                                  g           h
      |                 i                   2
 1.90 |              j     5
      |                    k
 1.00 |
      ---+-----+-----+-----+-----+-----+-----+-----+-----+-----+--
Perc02 1.0   1.6   2.2   2.8   3.4   4.0   4.6   5.2   5.8   6.4
```

LEGEND

		Ideal Points			
Label	Segment	Label	Brand	Label	Brand
1	1	a	SULI	f	SARK
2	2	b	SANE,SEMI	g	SULU
3	3	c	SALT	h	SONO
4	4	d	SIBI	i	SAMA
5	5	e	SOLD	j	SUSI
				k	SIAA

Graph 2

Period 8
Vertical Axis Variable:Perc01
Horizontal Axis Variable:Perc03

```
     Perc01
 7.00 |
      |
 6.10 |                                          a3 b        c
      |
 5.30 |                                             d  e
      |                                          4
 4.40 |                                    1
      |
 3.60 |
      |                                                    f
 2.70 |                                    g
      |                                       2     h
 1.90 |                                    i  5
      |                                          j
 1.00 |
      ---+-----+-----+-----+-----+-----+-----+-----+-----+-----+--
 Perc03 1.0   1.6   2.2   2.8   3.4   4.0   4.6   5.2   5.8   6.4
```

LEGEND

		Ideal Points			
Label	Segment	Label	Brand	Label	Brand
1	1	a	SULI	f	SARK
2	2	b	SEMI	g	SONO,SULU
3	3	c	SANE	h	SAMA
4	4	d	SIBI,SOLD	i	SUSI
5	5	e	SALT	j	SIAA

78

Graph 3

Period 8
Vertical Axis Variable:Perc02
Horizontal Axis Variable:Perc03

```
  Perc02
7.00 |
     |
6.10 |
     |                                     1   3   a           b
5.30 |                                         c   2   d       e
     |                                         f
4.40 |
     |
3.60 |                                         4   g
     |                                         5   h   i
2.70 |                                         j           k
     |
1.90 |
     |
1.00 |
     ---+-----+-----+-----+-----+-----+-----+-----+-----+-----+--
Perc03 1.0   1.6   2.2   2.8   3.4   4.0   4.6   5.2   5.8   6.4
```

LEGEND

	Ideal Points				
Label	Segment	Label	Brand	Label	Brand
1	1	a	SEMI	f	SULU
2	2	b	SANE	g	SIBI
3	3	c	SONO,SULI	h	SIAA
4	4	d	SOLD	i	SALT
5	5	e	SARK	j	SUSI
				k	SAMA

Exhibit 5.9

An Example Consultation with Advisor

The user first enters the name of the brand to be advertised, its product class, and the name of the targeted market segment into the Advisor template. He or she then checks off the objectives to be inferred. In the example shown below, the user has asked the system to determine the marketing and advertising objectives for brand SONO and target segment Singles.

OBJECTIVES ADVISOR

```
Brand name:SONO                          Product Class:Sonite

Target Audience:Singles

Select objectives to be determined
     Marketing Objective:x
     Advertising Objective:x
```

After the user "Escapes" from edit mode and selects the "Output" option, the system asks a series of questions about the situation. In the following text, each Advisor question is accompanied by a note describing the source of the answer (shown in boldface). The name of the analysis module and associated variables are shown in italics. This example assumes that the user has first run the Describe and Classify options to assign survey respondents to clusters, as described in Chapter 4.

```
What is the life cycle stage of Sonite?
Known values are
     1.   introduction
     2.   growth
     3.   maturity
     4.   decline
>> growth
```

* *Situation:Trend - UnitSales* of SONO are high while *UnitShare* is decreasing. This indicates that product category sales are increasing, and that Sonites are at the **growth** stage of the product life cycle.

```
What is the past product usage of Singles?
Known values are
    1.   none
    2.   some
>> none
```

* *Situation:Tabulate* - Most Singles (57 percent of Cluster 1) do not *OwnSonite*. Given the durability of the Sonite product, Singles who currently own a Sonite are probably not in the market to replace it. Therefore, we might choose to target our advertising at those Singles who do not own a Sonite. For this group, we might infer that Singles' past usage of Sonites is **none**. Of course, it is possible that Singles have used the Sonite of a friend or acquaintance, in which case we would report **some** product usage.

```
What is the current product usage of Singles?
Known values are
    1.   none
    2.   some
>> none
```

* See above.

```
What is the product type of SONO?
Known values are
    1.   existing brand
    2.   line extension of an existing brand
    3.   minor modification of an existing brand
    4.   major modification of an existing brand
    5.   new brand
>> 'existing brand'
```

* *Situation:Trend* - *UnitSales* of SONO were 75,000 in period 1, and have risen to 348,000 units in period 8. Therefore, SONO would be considered an **existing brand**. Note in the example above that user input with embedded spaces must be surrounded by single quotation marks. Alternatively, the user can type the number which is printed to the left of the desired response (e.g., 1).

```
What is the past brand usage of Singles?
Known values are
    1.   none
    2.   some
>> none
```

* See above.

```
What is the current brand usage of Singles?
Known values are
     1.   none
     2.   some
>> none
```

- See above.

```
What are the product category purchase motivations of Singles?
Known values are
     1.   problem removal
     2.   problem avoidance
     3.   product replacement
     4.   sensory stimulation
     5.   intellectual stimulation
     6.   social approval
     7.   self esteem
>> 4,6
```

- *Situation:Tabulate* - Fifty percent of Singles (Cluster 1) purchase products in the Sonite category *(CategMotiv)* for **sensory stimulation**, while 40 percent purchase them for **social approval**. A small group purchases the product for **intellectual stimulation**, but we can neglect this group for purposes of analysis. Category purchase motivation is a multi-valued variable. Therefore, the user can enter multiple responses, separated by commas.

```
What are the brand purchase motivations of Singles?
Known values are
     1.   problem removal
     2.   problem avoidance
     3.   dissatisfaction with current brand
     4.   sensory stimulation
     5.   intellectual stimulation
     6.   social approval
     7.   self esteem
>> 4,6
```

- *Situation:Tabulate* - Forty percent of Singles (Cluster 1) purchase a particular brand of Sonite *(BrandMotiv)* for **sensory stimulation**, while 50 percent purchase it for **social approval**.

```
What is the time of the brand decision for Singles?
Known values are
    1.   prior to purchase
    2.   at the time of purchase
>> 1
```

* *Situation:Tabulate* - Fifty four percent of Singles (Cluster 1) make their brand decisions *(DecisionTime)* outside of the store (i.e., **prior to purchase**), while the remaining 46 percent decide which brand to purchase within the store (**at the time of purchase**). In this example, we assume the first alternative. However, users should be encouraged to try both options to see how this affects the recommendations of the Advisor module.

```
What is the top-of-mind brand awareness of Singles?
Known values are
    1.   low
    2.   high
>> high
```

* *Objectives:ComAssess* - About 70 percent of Singles (Segment 2) have high top-of-mind **Awareness** of the SONO brand.

```
What is the product visibility at purchase of SONO?
Known values are
    1.   low
    2.   high
>> high
```

* Based on general knowledge of electronics products and their distribution outlets, we can assume that Sonites are prominently displayed at the point of purchase.

The output of the Advisor module is shown below. The instructor should emphasize to students that they should not blindly follow Advisor's recommendations. Instead, they should use the recommendations as one input, along with other ADSTRAT analyses and personal experiences, to guide the formulation of marketing and advertising objectives. For example, we learn from crosstabulating the variables *(Cluster)* and *(NecessSonite)* that 98 percent of Singles feel that it is necessary to own a Sonite. Therefore, it may not be necessary to stimulate primary demand, as recommended by the Advisor module.

OBJECTIVES ADVISOR

The marketing objectives of SONO are stimulate primary demand, and stimulate brand trial.

The value is stimulate primary demand because the product usage of Singles is none.

The value is stimulate brand trial because the brand usage of Singles is none.

....

The ad objectives of SONO are communicate brand image/mood/lifestyle, and communicate category image/mood/lifestyle, and maintain top-of-mind brand awareness.

The value is communicate brand image/mood/lifestyle because the marketing objective of SONO is stimulate brand trial, and the brand motivation direction of Singles is positive.

The value is communicate category image/mood/lifestyle because the marketing objective of SONO is stimulate primary demand, and the product motivation direction of Singles is positive.

The value is maintain top-of-mind brand awareness because the time of the brand decision for Singles is prior to purchase, and the top-of-mind brand awareness of Singles is high.

6

Budget Decisions

The budgeting decision discussion should be split into at least two sessions, as the material is more quantitative (assuming that the instructor chooses to develop these aspects). Transparencies covering these two sessions are included in Exhibit 6.1.

SESSION 1 consists of:

1. A discussion of the practice of advertising budgeting. The purpose is to show that a variety of different methods are used by managers and that, with the advent of computer technology, some better methods are becoming available.

2. The presentation of the Advertising to Sales ratio approach.

3. The description and discussion of marginal analysis based on the concept of advertising effectiveness or elasticity. This is followed by a demonstration of how to use the effectiveness option of the ADSTRAT budget module.

4. An evaluation of the two methods presented so far (AdToSales and Efficiency), in terms of which moderating communication factors are considered and how well they are considered. Figures 5.7 and 5.13 of the user's manual can be used to illustrate these points. This discussion sets the stage for the more complete BUDGET AID (ADBUDG) model.

SESSION 2 is devoted to the ADBUDG model (as implemented in ADSTRAT's BUDGET AID module), with a demonstration of how to decide on the inputs and how to interpret the slope values in the output. It is useful to demonstrate BUDGET AID in class using a brand and data from a past period. One of the transparencies in Exhibit 6.1 shows where the information necessary to run the model can be obtained using ADSTRAT. The brand used in this example is SIBI at Period 6 for Segment 4.

In the remaining pages of this chapter (and Exhibits 6.2 to 6.9), we will go through an example of how the various options of the budget module can be used to derive an advertising budget. This also demonstrates how different levels of complexity can be introduced to arrive at a budget recommendation. The brand that we will use for this example is SONO. The objective is to recommend an advertising budget for SONO in Period 9. The budget to be decided concerns the full year, although some allocation throughout the year is appropriate. (While there is no information avaiable in ADSTRAT on the seasonality of product sales, learning dynamics have an implication for the distribution of the budget over time. Consequently, we ask students to propose an advertising budget for the four quarters of Year 9.

From the AdToSales module output shown in Exhibit 6.2, it can be seen that SONO has the lowest advertising-to-sales ratio of the competitors (3.08 versus 4.66 and 7.50). SULU is the largest competitor and has the highest ratio of 7.50. This would suggest that if the decision were competitor-based, the advertising budget for SONO should be increased from the current $3,000,000. It should be noted, however, that the sales of SONO are the highest of all brands competing in this segment. Therefore, economies of scale would suggest that SONO should have a ratio lower than the competitors. Therefore, the current ratio of 3.08 is quite logical. Of course, this analysis does not consider how consumers react to changes in advertising spending. If consumers are relatively unresponsive (i.e., they have a low saturation point), then a lower level of advertising would be sufficient. If consumers are very responsive, higher spending would be justified.

The estimation of consumer responsiveness to advertising is complex. Advertising can affect various aspects of consumer behavior. First, advertising can affect primary demand (the segment unit sales). Next, advertising affects brand awareness. Then, advertising affects purchase intentions indirectly through awareness. Each of these relationships can be modeled in ADSTRAT. We now discuss these three models in turn. At the outset we should note that this is only one of a number of possible approaches for modeling advertising effectiveness with ADSTRAT.

The Primary Demand Effect of Advertising

The question here concerns the degree to which the advertising of SONO can change the segment sales. This can be estimated by regressing the segment size on the advertising expenditures. Because of the dynamics of demand, lagged segment sales should be used as a predictor variable. Of course, advertising is not the only determinant of the size of a segment. Price can also have an impact, depending on the elasticity of primary demand to price, and should therefore be included in the model.

One approach is to perform the analysis using information on just the SONO brand. The estimated model would indicate the ability of the advertising of SONO to affect the segment sales. Unfortunately, only eight observations are available for this analysis (one for each period). Consequently, the coefficients are not significant. (This run is not shown.) Assuming that each brand's advertising has the same effect on primary demand, we can pool the data for all brands to do the estimation. The cases selected are from Periods 1 to 8, including all brands, and selecting only data from Segment 2. The results appear in Exhibit 6.3. The equation for primary demand indicates that advertising and price do not significantly impact the size of Segment 2, although the coefficients are in the right direction (positive for advertising and negative for price). The coefficients are in fact similar to those obtained when using only the data from brand SONO. The same results are obtained when using a transformation for advertising and price to represent decreasing returns to scale. Therefore, we can conclude that the size of Segment 2 is not significantly affected by our advertising of SONO.

Given that our advertising does not seem to affect the segment size (primary demand), our focus then becomes the building of our brand's long-term market share. Because market share is affected by the availability of the product (which is a function of our production and distribution) and other factors which are not directly influenced by our advertising, it may be more appropriate to use purchase intentions as a surrogate measure of a brand's long-term share for advertising purposes. We will therefore concentrate on estimating the impact of advertising on purchase intentions. Data from all brands in Segment 2 over the eight periods are used in this analysis. The lagged purchase intention variable (Intent_Lg) is significant, indicating that there is a carry-over effect from the previous period. As in the earlier analysis of segment sales, advertising share has a positive coefficient and relative price has a negative coefficient, but these coefficients are not statistically significant (see Exhibit 6.4). This may be due to the misspecification of the model. One might hypothesize that advertising first operates to create brand awareness. Then, consumers' awareness of a brand's benefits leads to favorable purchase intentions. We now propose a recursive system of two equations to model these relationships.

The Awareness Model

Brand awareness is largely determined by the amount of brand advertising. However, competitors' advertising has a counter effect. This can be expressed in a parsimonious manner by representing our advertising as a share of voice in the market. This is the learning component of awareness. Because of the carry-over effects of past advertising, a lagged awareness variable should also be used to predict current awareness. If the brand is not advertised in a period, then awareness will drop by a certain amount due to forgetting. When we model these relationships using information from all the brands, we observe strongly significant parameters with an excellent fit ($R^2 = 0.951$), as shown in Exhibit 6.5. The model can be expressed as:

$$\text{Awareness}_{i,t} = 0.137 + 0.705 \ \text{Awareness}_{i,t-1} + 0.807 \ \text{Adshare}_{i,t}.$$

The logarithm of AdShare could be used to represent nonlinear effects. A multiplicative model cannot be used because this would indicate that Awareness will be zero if there is no advertising for a period, which is not logical.

The Purchase Intent Model

Purchase intent is, like market share, constrained to be between zero and one and should sum to one across brands in a given period. Therefore, the attraction model is appropriate for modeling purchase intentions. The attractiveness of a brand at a particular time is a function of how well consumers know the brand (brand awareness) and of the perceptions of the brand on the most important dimensions used to discriminate among brands, relative to their preferences (Dev01, Dev02, Dev03). It is clear that for a brand to be attractive, it must both be perceived as delivering the desired benefits and have a high awareness. Therefore a multiplicative functional form of attraction is appropriate. Consequently:

$$\text{Attraction}_{i,t} = e^{b_{0i}} \text{Awareness}_{i,t}^{b1} \text{Dev01}_{i,t}^{b2} \text{Dev02}_{i,t}^{b3} \text{Dev03}_{i,t}^{b4}$$

This model is estimated by selecting the corresponding variables as independent variables (i.e., Ln of Awareness, Ln of Dev01, Ln of Dev02, and Ln of Dev03). In addition, the variables Period and Brand are selected as well. This will create dummy variables for the brands and for the periods. There will be 7 dummies for the first seven periods, with the eighth period being part of the intercept. The period dummy variables are used to take into account the total attraction of all the brands, which varies by period. The dummy variables for each brand (excluding the last brand in the data set, which is included in the intercept) represent the fact that each brand has a specific (intrinsic) preference beyond the variables already in the model. It is not necessary to include these dummy variables. Without brand dummies, the intercept of the regression can be interpreted as the last period coefficient, assuming that the brand constants (b_{0i}) are equal to zero. In Exhibit 6.6, we included the brand dummies to represent the more typical case of the attraction model. The dependent variable is the logarithm of Purchase Intentions.

The results included in Exhibit 6.6 show significant effects of awareness and perceptions. The positive coefficient of Awareness (0.878) indicates that when awareness increases, purchase intentions increase as well. The negative signs of the deviation coefficients (-0.908, -0.763, and -0.202) indicate that, as the distance from the ideal point to the perceptions increases, the purchase intentions decrease (or that purchase intentions increase when the brand is perceived closer to the ideal brand for that segment). The fit is also very good, although this might be expected given the many dummy variables included in the model. The purchase intention model can therefore be expressed as:

$$\text{Intent}_{i,t} = \frac{\text{Attraction}_{i,t}}{\sum_{j=1}^{n} \text{Attraction}_{j,t}}$$

$$\text{Attraction}_{i,t} = e^{b_{0,i}} \text{Awareness}_{i,t}^{0.878} \text{Dev01}_{i,t}^{-0.908} \text{Dev02}_{i,t}^{-0.763} \text{Dev03}_{i,t}^{-0.202}$$

Marginal Analysis

If we consider purchase intentions to be indicative of the market share, the sales for brand i at time t can be written as:

$$S_{i,t} = SegSize_t \cdot Share_{i,t}$$

where:

$$Share_{i,t} = \frac{e^{b_{0i}} K_{i,t} \, Awareness_{i,t}^{0.878}}{\sum\limits_{j=1}^{n} e^{b_{0j}} K_{j,t} \, Awareness_{j,t}^{0.878}}$$

and where $K_{i,t}$ is the combined effect of Dev01, 02, and 03.

First, it is interesting to note that the elasticity of Share to Awareness is:

$$\varepsilon_{Awareness} = b_1(1 - Share)$$

This shows that, as the share gets closer to saturation, the awareness elasticity becomes smaller. This is the effect of the model specification which constrains the market share to be less than one.

The budgeting problem is to find the level of advertising ($Advert_{i,t}$) that maximizes profit. The profit function is:

$$\pi = S_{i,t} \, m_{i,t} - Advert_{i,t}$$

where
$S_{i,t}$ = Sales of brand i at time t,
$m_{i,t}$ = profit margin (price − cost),
$Advert_{i,t}$ = Advertising expenditures of the brand.

Expressing the profit equation as a function of market share of the brand (without subscripts):

$$\pi = SegSize \cdot Share \cdot m - Advert$$

Profits are maximized by setting the derivative of profits relative to advertising expenditures to zero:

$$\frac{\partial \pi}{\partial Advert} = SegSize \cdot m \cdot \frac{\partial Share}{\partial Awareness} \frac{\partial Awareness}{\partial AdShare} \frac{\partial AdShare}{\partial Advert} - 1 = 0$$

The derivatives are given below:

$$\frac{\partial Share}{\partial Awareness} = \frac{\beta_1}{Awareness} Share(1 - Share)$$

$$\frac{\partial Awareness}{\partial AdShare} = \alpha_2$$

and, assuming that the competitors' total advertising expenditures are represented by the constant "Them":

$$\frac{\partial AdShare}{\partial Advert} = \frac{Them}{(Them+Advert)^2}$$

Therefore:

$$SegSize \cdot m \frac{\beta_1}{Awareness} Share(1 - Share)\alpha_2 \frac{Them}{(Them+Advert)^2} = 1$$

89

Solving for Advert, the advertising expenditures of the brand:

$$(\texttt{Them+Advert})^2 = \texttt{SegSize} \cdot m \frac{\beta_1 \, \alpha_2}{\texttt{Awareness}} \texttt{Share}(1-\texttt{Share})\texttt{Them}$$

$$\texttt{Advert}^2 + 2\texttt{Advert} \cdot \texttt{Them} - \texttt{SegSize} \cdot m \frac{\beta_1 \, \alpha_2}{\texttt{Awareness}} \texttt{Share}(1-\texttt{Share})\,\texttt{Them} = 0$$

This equation can be solved for Advert. If one assumes that the competitors' total expenditures next period will be equal to their expenditures in the last period, Them = $33,400,000. The size of the segment (SegSize) is 690,000 units. The current Awareness level is 0.699. The margin is $189. The current market share is 0.351. Finally the model parameters β_1 and α_2 are respectively 0.878 and 0.807, as obtained from the estimations for Awareness_Lg and AdShare described above in Exhibits 6.6 and 6.5. Replacing the variables by their values, the equation becomes:

$$\texttt{Advert}^2 + 66.8 \times 10^6 \ \texttt{Advert} - 1.0058 \times 10^{15} = 0.$$

Solving this equation for Advert results in an optimal advertising budget of $6,329,112.

USING BUDGET AID

The BUDGET AID module allows students to enter alternative advertising budgeting scenarios and simulate the likely effects on brand sales and profitability. Example inputs to the option are shown in Exhibit 6.7. In the following discussion, we indicate how to derive the main inputs. For this example, we assume a period length of one year.

Advertising rate to maintain market share. According to the model, the market share is maintained if awareness does not change. For awareness not to change, it is necessary to spend some amount on advertising to compensate for forgetting. In fact, the AdShare necessary to maintain Share is found by setting Awareness$_t$ = Awareness$_{t-1}$ in the Awareness equation found in Exhibit 6.5:

$$\texttt{Awareness} = 0.137 + 0.705 \ \texttt{Awareness} = 0.807 \ \texttt{Adshare}$$

$$\texttt{Adshare} = [\texttt{Awareness}(1-0.705) - 0.137]/0.807.$$

Since Awareness is currently 0.699, the AdShare should be 0.086. Assuming that the advertising expenditures of the competitors remain the same at $33,400,000, this gives a maintenance budget of approximately $3,143,000. The advertising expenditures of each brand in Period 8 are obtained from the AdToSales option and total $36,400,000. Therefore, if we call our budget US and all other competitors' budget THEM, our AdShare is US/(THEM + US). Consequently, since US/(THEM + US) = 0.086,

$$\texttt{US} = \texttt{THEM} [0.086/(1-0.086)] = 33,400,000 [0.086/(1-0.086)] = 3,143,000.$$

Estimated market share at the end of period with zero advertising. This question can be answered by finding the brand awareness if there is no advertis-

90

ing (`AdShare` = 0) and by inserting this value in the purchase intention equation.
    If `AdShare` is zero, the Awareness equation becomes:

$$\texttt{Awareness}_t = 0.137 + 0.705\ \texttt{Awareness}_{t-1} = 0.137 + 0.705 \times 0.699 = 0.63.$$

A problem arises when inserting this value in the attraction equation to predict purchase intention. The brand dummy coefficients cannot be identified and the intercept contains the last period effect. This problem can, however, be solved as follows.
    Let:

$$\texttt{Share}_{i,t-1} = \frac{e^{b_{0i}}\ K_{i,t-1}}{TOT_{t-1}}$$

where

$$K_{i,t-1} = \texttt{Awareness}_{i,t-1}^{0.878}\ \texttt{Dev01}_{i,t-1}^{-0.908}\ \texttt{Dev02}_{i,t-1}^{-0.763}\ \texttt{Dev03}_{i,t-1}^{-0.202}$$

Given that the three Deviations values are 0.2, 0.39 and 0.6 respectively (as obtained from the Trend option of the Situation module), then $K_{i,t-1} = 7.10$. We know that the share (purchase intent) at Period $t-1$ is 0.351, so

$$TOT_{t-1} = \frac{7.10 e^{b_{0i}}}{.351} = 20.21 e^{b_{0i}}$$

Assuming that the competitors awareness and brand position relative to the ideal point do not change from Period $t-1$ to t, the total attraction (sum of the attractions of all the competitors) at Period t is:

$$TOT_t = TOT_{t-1} - e^{b_{0i}}\ K_{i,t-1} + e^{b_{0i}}\ K_{i,t}$$

If the perceptions of the brand (SONO) relative to the ideal point do not change, given the lower awareness of 0.63, it is possible to calculate $K_{i,t} = 6.48$. Therefore:

$$TOT_t = e^{b_{0i}}(20.21 - 7.10 + 6.48) = 19.59 e^{b_{0i}}$$

and $\texttt{Share}_{i,t} = 6.48/19.59 = 0.331$.
    Estimated market share at the end of period with the maintenance rate plus 20%. The same calculations as above can be done with advertising expenditures 20% over the maintenance rate of $3,143,000, i.e., with a budget of $3,771,000. This would be equivalent to an `AdShare` of 3,771,000/(33,400,000 + 3,771,000) = 0.1015 (assuming the total expenditures for the competitors is the same). With this `AdShare` value, the `Awareness` level is:

$$\texttt{Awareness} = 0.137 + (0.705 \times 0.699) + (0.807 \times 0.1015) = .712$$

The new value of $K_{i,t}$ can be computed:

$$K_{1,t} = (.712)^{0.878} \times 9.72 = 7.216$$

The total attraction is:

$$TOT_t = e^{b_{0i}}\ (20.21 - 7.10 + 7.216) = 20.33 e^{b_{0i}}$$

Therefore, the market Share would be

$$\text{Share}_{i,t} = 7.216 / 20.33 = .3555$$

Estimated market share at the end of period with saturation advertising. With saturation advertising, awareness will be maximum at 100%. In this case, replacing awareness by 1.0, $K_{i,t} = 9.72$, and

$$\text{TOT}_t = e^{b_{0i}} (20.21 - 7.10 + 9.72) = 22.83 e^{b_{0i}}$$

The market share is then:

$$\text{Share}_{i,t} = 9.72 / 22.83 = 0.426.$$

Long-run market share. The market share if the brand is never advertised in the long run can be set to zero or to a small number such as 10%.

Average brand price. We assume that the price of the brand will not change from Period 8 to 9. The price at Period 8 is found in the trend option to be $340.

Contribution Profit. This is the price minus the cost, which is found using the trend option to be $151.

Product class sales. The size of Segment 2 is 690,000 at Period 8 (as per the trend option). We assume that the market size will remain constant in Period 9.

Average product price. Given that the other two brands selling to this segment are $325 and $310 and that we are selling at $340, we can set the average at approximately $325.

FINDING THE OPTIMAL BUDGET

We can now run the model with a starting value of advertising expenditures. If the value of the slope is positive, this indicates that profits can be increased by increasing the level of advertising. We therefore increase this value until the slope approaches zero. This optimal condition is found for a budget of $4,000,000, an increase from the current advertising rate (see Exhibit 6.8). Note that this budget differs from the results obtained with the marginal analysis. This is due to differences in model specifications. For example, the model used for marginal analysis exhibits decreasing returns to scales only, while BUDGET AID's response function can be S-shaped with increasing and decreasing returns to scale. Also, the BUDGET AID model explicitly recognizes carry-over effects which were not taken into consideration for the marginal analysis.

In this example, the number of periods was set to one year. Alternatively, the budget could be evaluated for four periods of one quarter each. This requires changing some of the parameters in the response function and the advertising maintenance rate. The advertising maintenance rate is simply divided by four since there is no seasonality in this product category, giving a value of $786,000 per quarter. We can estimate that, with zero advertising, the drop in market share would be approximately $(35.1 - 33.1)/4 = 0.5$ share points per quarter, assuming a linear decline. Therefore, the market share at the end of the first period with no advertising would be 34.6%. For the maintenance rate plus 20% advertising level, the gain in share would be $(35.6 - 35.1)/4 = 0.125$ points during the first period, which gives a share of 35.25%. The saturation level does not change.

The product class sales per period are also divided by 4, which gives 172,500 units per quarter. By dividing the planning horizon into four quarters, the instructor can demonstrate that, because of the response function dynamics, it is more profitable to advertise early rather than later. The results of this analysis are shown in Exhibit 6.9. The recommended budget decreases over the planning horizon. This is in part due to the fact that there are no profits to be made after the planning horizon. In fact, this effect is attenuated if the model is run over eight periods (i.e., for the next two years), thereby showing the end-game phenomenon.

In summary, we have shown how the different options in ADSTRAT can be used to help derive the advertising budget. We have illustrated how each option builds on the other from a simple method to a more complete approach.

Exhibit 6.1

Transparencies
for
Budget Decisions

BUDGET DECISION
Session 1

ADVERTISING BUDGET DECISION

1.   The Budgeting Methods

2.   Advertising to Sales Ratio

3.   Methods based on Advertising Effectiveness

1. WHAT ARE THE METHODS USED FOR DETERMINING THE ADVERTISING BUDGET?

- All you can afford

- Competitive Parity

- % of Past Year's Sales

- % of Anticipated Sales

- Objective and Task

PERCENT OF RESPONDENTS USING EACH METHOD

Method	Consumer Goods	Industrial Goods
Affordable	20%	33%
Arbitrary	4	13
Match Competitors	24	21
Objective/Task	63	74
% of Anticipated Sales	53	16
% of Past Year's Sales	20	23
Per unit of sales	21	2
Quantitative	51	3

Note: Percentages do not sum to 100% because some respondents reported using more than one method.

2. ADVERTISING TO SALES RATIO

3. METHOD BASED ON ADVERTISING EFFECTIVENESS

Marginal Analysis

ADSTRAT: An Advertising Decision Support System

ESTIMATING CONSUMER RESPONSE TO ADVERTISING

- Experimentation

- Econometric Analysis

- Managerial Judgment

ESTIMATING THE SALES RESPONSE FUNCTION WITH AN ECONOMETRIC ANALYSIS

- Time Series Analysis

- Cross-Sectional Analysis

- Time Series and Cross-Sectional Analysis

REGRESSION ANALYSIS

- Dependent Variable?

- Independent Variables?

- Shape of Relationship?

- Competitive Effects?

COMPETITIVE EFFECTS
Market Share Models

How can we take competition into account in a regression model?

Constraints on Market Share Models:

- Market Share should be between 0 and 1

- Market Shares for all the brands should total to 1

Attraction Model

QUANTITY OF ADVERTISING
= REACH & FREQUENCY

- Distribution of Number of Exposures

- Gross Rating Points

- Timing Effects

MODELING LEARNING & FORGETTING

- Lagged Dependent Variable as Independent Variable

- Long Term Advertising Effects: The Koyck Model

EVALUATION OF

- Advertising to Sales Ratio Method

- Econometric Analysis

BUDGET DECISION

Session 2

WHAT ARE THE FACTORS AFFECTING
THE BUDGETING DECISION?

The effectiveness of advertising expenditures (exposures) depends on:

- copy

- media

- learning rate

- forgetting rate

- seasonality

WHY IS A MODEL USEFUL?

- The real phenomenon is complex and ill-structured.

- Every decision maker uses a model (intuitive or formal) to help structure and solve a problem.

What is a Model?

A model is a simplified, formal representation of a real phenomenon.

It is the choice of a set of variables and the specification of their inter-relationships designed to represent some real system or process.

BUDGET AID:
A DECISION AID MODEL

A model-based set of procedures for processing data and judgments to assist a manager in his or her decision making.

The model is:

- simple,

- robust,

- easy to control,

- adaptive,

- complete on important issues,

- easy to communicate with.

BUDGET AID:
AN IMPLEMENTATION OF ADBUDG

Three components:

1.   The brand's long-run market share without advertising,

2.   The carryover effects of past advertising,

3.   The incremental effect of current advertising.

THE INCREMENTAL EFFECT OF CURRENT ADVERTISING

1. If advertising is cut to zero, market share will not fall below min.

2. If advertising is increased to infinity (saturation), market share will not be larger than max.

3. The response function of market share to advertising is either concave or S-shaped.

Therefore, the response function is:

$$\text{Min} + (\text{Max} - \text{Min}) \frac{\text{Adv}_t^{\gamma}}{\delta + \text{Adv}_t^{\gamma}}$$

where the advertising rate, adv_t, is:

$$\text{Adv}_t = \text{Advert}_t \times \text{Copy}_t \times \text{Media}_t$$

CARRYOVER EFFECTS

- A percentage (persistence) of last period share is retained:

$$\text{persist} \; (\text{share}_{t-1} - \text{longmin})$$

- Persistence is defined as:

$$\text{persist} = \frac{\text{min} - \text{longmin}}{\text{initialshare} - \text{longmin}}$$

THE FULL MODEL

$\text{Share}_t = \text{longmin}$

$$+ \frac{\text{min} - \text{longmin}}{\text{initialshare} - \text{longmin}} \ (\text{Share}_{t-1} - \text{longmin})$$

$$+ (\text{max} - \text{min}) \ \frac{\text{Adv}_t^{\gamma}}{\delta + \text{Adv}_t^{\gamma}}$$

USING BUDGET AID:
A Demonstration

BRAND: SIBI
PERIOD: 6
SEGMENT: 4

Market Share:	71.6% (ComAssess)
Ad Expenditures:	$4,500,000 (Trends or AdToSales in '000s)
Price:	$400 (Trends)
Cost:	$75 (Trends)
Product class sales:	800,000 units (Trends in '000s)
Relative Price:	1.1 (Trends in '000s)
Contribution Profit:	$400 - $75 = $325
Average product price:	$400/1.1 = $364
Unit sales:	.716 x 800,000 = 572,800
Dollar sales:	572,800 x $400 = $229,120,000

USING BUDGET AID

1. Each time period should represent one quarter.

2. Reproduce, as best as you can, the market share results from previous period(s).

3. Update the model based on year-to-date results (e.g. media, copy etc.).

4. Evaluate new strategies with different budgeting plans.

Exhibit 6.2

```
Output from Module:Budget:AdToSales        ADSTRAT Version 1.0
Dataset: indup.dat                         Copyright 1991, 1992

Mon Apr 27 17:10:16 1992                    H. Gatignon & R. Burke
```

ADVERTISING TO SALES

Brand	Advertising (in thousand $)				Period
	6	7	8	Total	
sark	1900	0	1800	3700	
sono	2500	2000	3000	7500	
sulu	5000	3000	4000	12000	

Brand	Sales (Revenues - in thousand $)				Period
	6	7	8	Total	
sark	22022	22022	33582	77625	
sono	55454	91220	118320	264994	
sulu	40701	61865	74340	176906	

Brand	Ratio (as % of sales)				Period
	6	7	8	Avg.	
sark	8.63	0.00	5.36	4.66	
sono	4.51	2.19	2.54	3.08	
sulu	12.28	4.85	5.38	7.50	

Exhibit 6.3

```
Output from Module:Budget:Effectiveness      ADSTRAT Version 1.0
Dataset: indup.dat,panel.dat                 Copyright 1991, 1992

Parameter file:                              H. Gatignon & R. Burke
Mon Apr 27 17:12:54 1992
```

MEASURING ADVERTISING EFFECTIVENESS

OLS Analysis
Dependent variable: SegSize

Source	Df	Sum of squares	Mean Square	F value	R square
Model	3	1.5e+006	4.99e+005	51.874	0.658
Error	81	7.79e+005	9620		
Total	84	2.28e+006			

Parameter	Estimate	Standard Error	t value
Intercept	148	49	3.02
Price	-0.0131	0.0909	-0.144
Advert	0.0052	0.00446	1.17
SegSize_Lg	0.785	0.0635	12.4

```
Output from Module:Budget:Effectiveness     ADSTRAT Version 1.0
Dataset: indup.dat,panel.dat                Copyright 1991, 1992

Parameter file:                             H. Gatignon & R. Burke
Mon Apr 27 17:14:46 1992
```

MEASURING ADVERTISING EFFECTIVENESS

OLS Analysis
Dependent variable: Intent

Source	Df	Sum of squares	Mean Square	F value	R square
Model	3	0.369	0.123	19.192	0.415
Error	81	0.519	0.00641		
Total	84	0.888			

Parameter	Estimate	Standard Error	t value
Intercept	0.0432	0.0367	1.18
AdShare	0.161	0.139	1.16
RelPrice	-0.039	0.0298	-1.31
Intent_Lg	0.807	0.125	6.47

Exhibit 6.5

```
Output from Module:Budget:Effectiveness      ADSTRAT Version 1.0
Dataset: indup.dat,panel.dat                 Copyright 1991, 1992

Mon Apr 27 17:16:16 1992                      H. Gatignon & R. Burke
```

MEASURING ADVERTISING EFFECTIVENESS

OLS Analysis
Dependent variable: Awareness

Source	Df	Sum of squares	Mean Square	F value	R square
Model	2	1.41	0.706	792.482	0.951
Error	82	0.073	0.00089		
Total	84	1.48			

Parameter	Estimate	Standard Error	t value
Intercept	0.137	0.0135	10.2
AdShare	0.807	0.0531	15.2
Awareness_Lg	0.705	0.0223	31.6

Exhibit 6.6

```
Output from Module:Budget:Effectiveness          ADSTRAT Version 1.0
Dataset: indup.dat,panel.dat                     Copyright 1991, 1992
Parameter file:                                  H. Gatignon & R. Burke
Mon Apr 27 17:23:59 1992
```

MEASURING ADVERTISING EFFECTIVENESS

OLS Analysis
Dependent variable: Intent_Ln

Source	Df	Sum of squares	Mean Square	F value	R square
Model	27	148	5.5	35.151	0.928
Error	74	11.6	0.156		
Total	101	160			

Parameter	Estimate	Standard Error	t value
Intercept	-3.96	0.254	-15.6
Awareness_Ln	0.878	0.276	3.18
Dev01_Ln	-0.908	0.103	- 8.78
Dev02_Ln	-0.763	0.104	- 7.32
Dev03_Ln	-0.202	0.0753	- 2.68
Period_D01	2.82	0.206	13.7
Period_D02	2.65	0.201	13.2
Period_D03	2.03	0.177	11.5
Period_D04	1.84	0.172	10.7
Period_D05	1.62	0.166	9.76
Period_D06	-0.167	0.156	- 1.07
Period_D07	0.285	0.16	1.78
Brand_D01	0.291	0.292	0.996
Brand_D02	-0.55	0.211	- 2.61
Brand_D03	-0.234	0.365	- 0.642
Brand_D04	0.205	0.263	0.78
Brand_D05	-0.686	0.538	- 1.28
Brand_D06	0.552	0.288	1.91
Brand_D07	-0.28	0.333	- 0.842
Brand_D08	1	0.481	2.08
Brand_D09	0.117	0.299	0.39
Brand_D10	0.214	0.292	0.732
Brand_D11	-0.224	0.222	- 1.01
Brand_D12	-0.326	0.342	- 0.952
Brand_D13	-0.76	0.374	- 2.03
Brand_D14	0.68	0.218	3.12
Brand_D15	-0.344	0.34	- 1.01
Brand_D16	0.946	0.33	2.86

BUDGET AID

Brand Data

Number of time periods (1 to 12): 1
Market share in period previous to period #1 (% of units): 35.10
Market share at the start of period #1 (% of units): 35.10
Advertising rate to maintain this market share ($/period): 3143000.00
Estimated market share at the end of period #1 (% of units) . . .
        with zero advertising: 33.10
        with the maintenance rate plus 20%: 35.60
        with saturation advertising: 42.60
Long run market share with zero advertising (% of units): 0.00
Average brand price ($/unit): 340.00
Contribution profit (before advertising expense) ($/unit): 189.00

Product Class Data

Product class sales at the start of period #1 (units): 690000.00
Average product price ($/unit): 325.00

Consider response to product class advertising?: __
(If checked, enter the following information)
Advertising rate to maintain product class sales ($/period):_____
Product class sales at the end of period #1 (units) . . .
        with zero advertising: _____
        with the maintenance rate plus 20%:   _____
        with saturation advertising: _____
Long run product class sales with zero advertising (units):_____

Seasonal and Trend Factors

Check the following factors that vary over time

                    Maintenance advertising rate: __
      Non-advertising effects on brand share: __
                        Product class sales: __
                            Media efficiency: __
                        Copy effectiveness: __

(Enter index values for items checked above; average = 1.00)

Period	1	2	3	4	5	6	7	8	9	10	11	12
Maintenc.adv.rate	:	:	:	:	:	:	:	:	:	:	:	
Brand share	:	:	:	:	:	:	:	:	:	:	:	
Product class sales	:	:	:	:	:	:	:	:	:	:	:	
Media efficiency	:	:	:	:	:	:	:	:	:	:	:	
Copy efficiency	:	:	:	:	:	:	:	:	:	:	:	

Brand Advertising

Advertising rate ($/period)

1	2	3	4	5	6
4000000.00:	:	:	:	:	

7	8	9	10	11	12
:	:	:	:	:	

Index of overall media efficiency   (average = 1.00): 1.00
Index of overall copy effectiveness (average = 1.00): 1.00

Exhibit 6.8

```
Output from Module:Budget:BudgetAid          ADSTRAT Version 1.0
Dataset: None                                Copyright 1991, 1992

Parameter file:                              H. Gatignon & R. Burke
Mon Apr 27 17:27:08 1992
```

BUDGET AID

Period	Share	Brand Sales		Product Sales	
		Units	Dollars	Units	Dollars
	(%)	(000s)	(000s)	(000s)	(000s)
------	-----	-------	-------	-------	--------
1	35.78	247	83934	690	224250

Total Sales $83933704.49 / 246864 Units
Total Product Sales $130410000.00 / 690000 Units

Period	Contrib before advert (000s)	Advertising cost (000s)	Contrib after advert (000s)	Cumul contrib (000s)	Slope
------	-------	-------	-------	-------	------
1	46657.27	4000	42657.27	42657.27	-0.00

Total Cost 4000000.00 Dollars

Exhibit 6.9

Output from Module:Budget:BudgetAid   ADSTRAT Version 1.0
Dataset: None   Copyright 1991, 1992

Parameter file: H. Gatignon & R. Burke
Mon Apr 27 17:30:53 1992

BUDGET AID

Period	Share	Brand Sales		Product Sales	
		Units	Dollars	Units	Dollars
	(%)	(000s)	(000s)	(000s)	(000s)
1	38.15	66	22375	173	56062
2	39.69	68	23278	173	56062
3	39.12	67	22947	173	56062
4	38.57	67	22620	173	56062

Total Sales $91220497.75 / 268296 Units
Total Product Sales $130410000.00 / 690000 Units

Period	Contrib before advert (000s)	Advertising cost (000s)	Contrib after advert (000s)	Cumul contrib (000s)	Slope
1	12438.10	3900	8538.10	8538.10	-0.00
2	12940.04	2300	10640.04	19178.14	-0.00
3	12755.71	0	12755.71	31933.86	-0.92
4	12574.01	0	12574.01	44507.86	-0.96

Total Cost 6200000.00 Dollars

7

Media Decisions

In this chapter, we first describe the content of a typical class session by reviewing the transparencies provided at the end of this chapter (Exhibit 7.1). Then, we go through an example of how to derive a media plan with ADSTRAT, using the decisions described in the preceding chapters as a foundation.

CONTENT OF A CLASS SESSION

Media planning involves four types of decisions. These decisions are outlined at the beginning of the class session (see the first transparency of Exhibit 7.1). They are:

Media class decisions, which concern the choice of one or more channels of communication, such as television, radio, magazine, or newspaper;

Media vehicle decisions, which determine the placement of ads in specific communication outlets, such as particular TV shows or magazines;

Media option decisions, which concern the ad's media characteristics, such as size, length, and color of the ad; and,

Media timing decisions, which determine the scheduling of media options over time.

It is useful to spend some time defining the major concepts used in media planning. These definitions are also included in the transparencies:

Ad Insertion: The placement of a single advertisement in a specific media vehicle and option at a certain point in time.

Audience: The number of people or households who are exposed to a media vehicle.

Frequency: The number of times an audience is exposed to the advertisement over a certain time period.

Reach: The number of different people who are exposed to a particular media vehicle at least once during a certain time period.

Effective Reach: The percentage of a vehicle's audience that belongs to the target market.

Coverage: The fraction of people in a target market who are in the audience of a given vehicle.

When defining the notion of frequency of exposures, it is useful to draw a bar graph of a typical distribution of exposures. For example, over a four-week period, a prime time TV campaign can generate a reach of 75% (25% are not exposed to the ad), 21% are exposed once, 18% are exposed twice, 13% are exposed three times, 8% are exposed four times, 5% are exposed five times, 3% are exposed six times, 2% are exposed seven times and 5% are exposed eight times or more. From such a graph, it is easier for students to understand the notions of reach and of repetition of exposures. It is also useful to define Gross Rating Points as the percentage of individuals who have been exposed to the ad at least once (Reach) times the average frequency of exposure.

The definitions of Effective Reach and Coverage are best illustrated by drawing a Ven diagram. One circle represents the audience set A and another one represents the target set T. The two circles intersect and their intersection represents individuals who are in the audience of a vehicle and who are in the targeted market. Then, it is easy to define effective reach as the conditional probability of being in the target given that the individual is in the audience $(A \cap T/A)$. Market coverage is defined as the conditional probability of being in the audience, given that the individual is in the target $(A \cap T/T)$.

After this introduction, it is useful to ask students what factors need to be considered when making media decisions. This leads to a discussion of Figure 7.1 in the ADSTRAT user's manual. This serves as an introduction to the three options in the media module in ADSTRAT by providing a framework to evaluate each option.

The Cost-per-thousand option is the simplest of the media planning tools. The ADSTRAT output shows the cost of an insertion, the audience size and the cost-per-thousand for the vehicles selected. This option can be used to introduce students to the concept of vehicle efficiency and the cost-per-thousand measure. This should be the first step of any analysis since those vehicles which are too high in cost-per-thousand should probably be eliminated from further analysis. The objective of this step is to narrow down the number of vehicles to evaluate further. One problem with this method is that the cost-per-thousand numbers can be misleading because they are based on total audience size. For example, a vehicle i could have a low cost-per-thousand, which compares favorably to another vehicle j (which has a higher cost-per-thousand). However, the audience of vehicle i might not correspond to the target while vehicle j provides a perfect match. Therefore, in such a case, when effective reach is taken into consideration, vehicle j would be preferable to vehicle i. The cost-per-thousand information does not tell us how well the vehicle reaches the target audience. Consequently, this analysis should be used to eliminate only the highest cost-per-thousand vehicles, because they are most likely to be inefficient options. Students should also be cautioned against comparing cost-per-thousand estimates across media classes because of differences in the nature of the communication experience.

Linear programming does take into consideration the notion of effective reach. ADSTRAT's linear programming (Allocation) option allocates the media budget so as to maximize the number of "effective" ad exposures. If the default values for the three factors of exposure probability, effective rach, and option effect are used, then the Allocation module selects vehicles based on which alternatives have the lowest cost-per-thousand. (In some cases, it cannot select the lowest cost-per-thousand vehicle because the insertion cost would cause the total budget to exceed the budget constraint, so it selects a less efficient and less costly alternative. This is a minor effect which only occurs with the last few insertions.) If instead, we enter the actual values of effective reach, then the Allocation option picks vehicles which most efficiently reach the target audience. These effective reach measures can be obtained by cross-tabulating the cluster representing the target segment with the media readership or viewership categories included in the survey (SURVEY.DAT), as described in the user's manual and as illustrated below. Of course, the other two factors (exposure probability and option effect) can be used as well, although these figures would have to be estimated subjectively by the user based on his or her personal knowledge of the media vehicles. The exposure probability concerns the probability of seeing the ad (of being exposed to the ad) given that the individual is in the audience. The option effect represents the quality of the exposure, or the degree of the match between the product or brand and the vehicle.

Finally, the Media Aid option takes into consideration the same factors, but in addition, it enables the development of a media schedule over time. For that purpose, it takes into account learning (frequency of exposure) and forgetting effects over time. The transparencies at the end of this chapter (Exhibit 7.1) present a step-by-step description of the MEDIAC model and show how to estimate the model's parameters. The last transparency in Exhibit 7.1 provides a description of the media scheduling process. We now follow this process in order to illustrate how the ADSTRAT media module options can be used to develop a media plan for the next twelve months (Period 9).

DEVELOPMENT OF A MEDIA PLAN

Continuing with the earlier example, the media plan will be developed for brand SONO, and will be targeted at Segment 2 with a budget of $6,000,000. (Recall that the optimal budget was found to be between $4 million and $6 million). The budget will be allocated to specific vehicles for each of the twelve months of Period (year) 9.

1. *Segmentation and Target Selection*

As indicated above, we have chosen to target Segment 2.

2. *Eliminate certain media and/or vehicles which are obviously inappropriate on qualitative dimensions.*

The media class and creative strategy decisions must be coordinated. On the one hand, given the technical nature of the Sonite product, we might limit advertising to print media because of their ability to communicate complex product information. On the other hand, we might have a creative strategy which focuses on a single product benefit, and can be successfully executed in broadcast media. For purposes of this example, we will consider both print and broadcast media for inclusion.

3. *Analyze vehicles left based on coverage and cost information and proceed to further elimination of vehicles.*

We can first screen out those vehicles with very high cost-per-thousand values. This information is obtained by running the cost-per-thousand option with all the vehicles selected. The results are shown in Exhibit 7.2. Vehicles with costs-per-thousand above 30 or 40 can be tentatively eliminated based on low efficiency. (If we later determine that these vehicles have a high effective reach, we might reconsider this decision.)

Another method for identifying the most cost efficient vehicles is to run the Allocation module. This option automatically selects the lowest cost-per-thousand alternatives until the budget constraint is reached. This is shown in the output of the media allocation option (Exhibit 7.3) where the three indices (exposure probability, effective reach, and option effect) are set to 1.00.

The next step is to identify those vehicles which most efficiently reach target Segment 2. The coverage and effective reach information are obtained by cross-tabulating vehicle readership and cluster membership. Recalling that the cluster corresponding to Segment 2 is Cluster 1, cross tabulations are performed as shown in Exhibits 7.4 and 7.5 for the ReadFashion and WtchDayTV variables. The vehicles that are seen or read most by the target audience (highest coverage) can be retained in the media plan. The coverage information appears in the cross-tab table as the row percentage for the column labeled "1" and the row corresponding to the cluster of interest. For example, Exhibit 7.4, indicates that 84.62% of Cluster 1 (Segment 2) reads fashion magazines. The specific vehicles in the fashion category appear in Table 2.6 of the user's manual.

For the most promising alternatives (vehicles with the highest efficiency and coverage), we enter the effective reach, exposure probability, and option effect information into the media allocation module. The effective reach information is obtained from the same cross-tabulation tables used earlier. This time, however, we use the column percentage for the column labeled "1" and the row matching the cluster of interest. For example, *Glamour* magazine, which is a fashion magazine, has an effective reach of 26.83% or 0.27 (Exhibit 7.4). For national daytime TV programming, the effective reach is 19.61% or 0.20 (Exhibit 7.5).

In addition to the effective reach, we consider that black and white advertisements in magazines might not be noticed as often as color advertisements. We subjectively estimate that they will be seen with a probability of 0.5, that is, half as often as a color ad. The exception is *TV Guide*, where individuals may be less likely to flip past a black and white ad since they are looking for program information. (Therefore, a probability of 0.7 is used.) Of course, you are free to use a different set of exposure probabilities depending on your assumptions concerning audience response. Finally, the probabilities of being exposed to the ad for day time TV are assumed to be lower than for print advertising, with values respectively of 0.2 and 0.3 for national daytime TV and for national early news on TV. We assume a higher level of audience involvement for the other TV shows, so the exposure probabilities are set equal to color advertisements in magazines. For purposes of this example, we consider the option effect to be the same across all these vehicles. The maximum number of insertions is 12 (although more than one insertion per month could be specified for the TV programs).

This leads to the results shown in Exhibit 7.6, where the only TV show selected is Golden Girls. All other insertions are in magazines.

4. *Schedule ad insertions for remaining vehicles*

The Media Aid option is used for the ad scheduling analysis. The inputs and outputs are shown in Exhibits 7.7 and 7.8 respectively. As indicated, the budget is set at $6,000,000. The analysis is performed for a planning period of twelve months. The target audience for SONO is Segment 2. Information on Segment 2 is entered into the first column of the population and effective reach tables. The eight vehicles suggested in the previous allocation analysis are used in MEDIA AID, and are numbered 1 through 8.

The input for the response function is subjectively determined. We assume that, with saturation advertising, 100% of the audience's purchase potential would be realized. The other values should be based on the students' rationale for a learning or a low involvement situation. Also, due to the uncertainty of this response function, sensitivity analysis should be performed. The values entered for this illustration are 0 for no exposure, 30 for a single exposure value and 80 for an exposure value of 3.

The population corresponds to the number of units potentially sold in Segment 2 with saturation advertising. We indicated in the budgeting chapter that the market share in this case would be 0.426. Given that the segment size is 690,000 units, the potential sales are 690,000 × 0.426, which we rounded up to 295,000. Alternatively, the segment size figure could be used as the potential unit sales with saturation advertising. This is clearly an upper limit, and may be overly optimistic in face of strong competition. The potential sales per individual is the price of the brand, i.e., $340 for brand SONO.

The memory constant is set at 0.75, following the research results reported in the ADSTRAT student manual (page 139).

The inputs for the exposure value, exposure probability, and effective reach parameters are the same as those used in the Allocation option and explained above. Finally, the cost and audience data are obtained from the cost-per-thousand option discussed above. The maximum number of insertions per period is simply the frequency of publication of the vehicle, which is given in the ADSTRAT student manual in Table 2.6. Therefore, for a weekly publication, four insertions per month would be considered the maximum number of insertions.

The results indicate that the bulk of the advertising should be placed in vehicles 2, 3, 4 and 7, which correspond to JetBW, Jet4C, PeopleBW and NatlEnq4C. The system recommends placing more ads early in the schedule to take advantage of the carry-over effects of advertising. The model could be rerun to avoid having 8 insertions per month in Jet (4 B&W and 4 in color). This could be done by specifying a maximum number of insertions of two for each alternative (JetBW and Jet4C) or by eliminating one of these options.

Exhibit 7.1

Transparencies
for
Media Decisions

MEDIA PLANNING
Four types of decisions

- MEDIA CLASS DECISIONS: the choice of one or more channels of communication, such as television, radio, magazine, or newspaper.

- MEDIA VEHICLE DECISIONS: the placement of ads in specific communication outlets, such as particular TV shows or magazines.

- MEDIA OPTION DECISIONS: the determination of the ad's media characteristics, such as size, length, and color of the ad.

- TIMING DECISIONS: the scheduling of media options over time.

ADVERTISING MEDIA TERMINOLOGY

- AD INSERTION: The placement of a single advertisement in a specific media vehicle and option at a certain point in time.

- AUDIENCE: The number of people or households who are exposed to a media vehicle.

- FREQUENCY: The number of times an audience is exposed to the advertisement over a certain time period.

ADVERTISING MEDIA TERMINOLOGY
(Continued)

- REACH: The number of different people who are exposed to a particular media vehicle at least once during a certain time period.

- EFFECTIVE REACH: The percentage of a vehicle's audience that belongs to the target market.

- COVERAGE: The fraction of people in a target market who are in the audience of a given vehicle.

MEDIA AND SCHEDULING DECISIONS MODULE

- Media Efficiency: Cost-per-thousand

- Media Allocation: Linear Programming

- Media Aid: A Decision Aid Model

MEDIA EFFICIENCY: Cost-per-thousand

Information required:

- Audience size

- Cost per insertion

$$\text{Cost-per-thousand} \ = \ \frac{(\text{Cost per insertion} \times 1000)}{\text{Audience Size}}$$

MEDIA ALLOCATION: LINEAR PROGRAMMING

Objective:

Maximize the number of persons exposed, subject to a budget constraint.

Basic Formulation:

$$\text{Max} \quad r_1x_1 + r_2x_2 + \ldots + r_jx_j + \ldots + r_nx_n$$
$$\text{s.t.} \quad c_1x_1 + c_2x_2 + \ldots + c_jx_j + \ldots + c_nx_n < B$$

where

$r_j = $ number of individuals reached with 1 insertion in vehicle j,

$x_j = $ number of insertions in vehicle j,

$c_j = $ cost of 1 insertion in vehicle j,

$B = $ Total media budget.

ADSTRAT MODIFICATION
TO LINEAR PROGRAMMING

Effectiveness Rating = function of

- Exposure probability
  (Probability of being exposed to ad)

- Effective Reach
  (Proportion of audience which is in target)

- Option effect
  (match product/vehicle)

$$\text{Max } e_1 r_1 x_1 + e_2 r_2 x_2 + ... + e_j r_j x_j + ... + e_n r_n x_n$$

$e_j =$ Product of the three indices (each index being between 0 and 1)

LIMITATIONS OF LINEAR PROGRAMMING

- Linearity assumption

  ◦ each additional insertion has the same effect,

  ◦ each additional insertion costs the same amount.

- No audience duplication

- No information about scheduling

MEDIA AID: A DECISION AID MODEL
MEDIAC

For a segment s at time t,

- 1 insertion in vehicle j should have a certain effect:

$$d_{sjt}$$

- x insertions:

$$d_{sjt} \, x_{jt}$$

- The effect of advertising in all media vehicles j = 1,....J:

$$\Sigma \, d_{sjt} \, x_{jt}$$

This is the effect of the current advertising.

MEDIAC (continued)

- Advertising from the previous period has some residual effect:

$$y_{st} = \alpha\, y_{s(t-1)} + \Sigma\, d_{sjt}\, x_{jt}$$

where

y_{st} = exposure value per capita in segment s at time t.

- What is the effect of an insertion in vehicle j at time t for someone in segment s, i.e., what is d_{sjt}?

$$d_{sjt} = h_j\, g_{sj}\, k_{jt}\, e_j$$

where:

h_j = probability of exposure to ad,
g_{sj} = market coverage, i.e., probability of being in audience of j given that the person is in segment s,
k_{jt} = seasonal index of audience,
e_j = media option source effect.

Note: This implementation of MEDIAC does not model duplication of audiences

MEDIAC (continued)

• Then, Sales are a function of the exposure value:

$$S_{st} = N_s \, m_{st} \, g(y_{st})$$

where:

N_s = Potential unit sales in segment s

m_{st} = Price of brand being analyzed (in segment s) at time t.

$g(\cdot)$ = response function

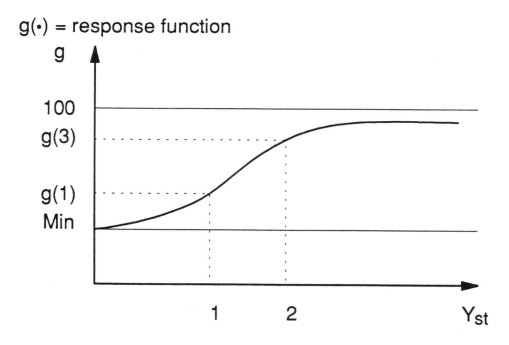

MARKET COVERAGE VERSUS EFFECTIVE REACH

MEDIA VEHICLE
READERSHIP

		NO	YES	
SEGMENTING VARIABLE (CLUSTER)	Cluster 1			
	Cluster 2		n_3	
	Cluster 3			
	Cluster 4			
	Cluster 5	n_1	n_2	Individuals in segment
			Individuals in audience	

$$g = n_2 / (n_1 + n_2)$$
$$r = n_2 / (n_2 + n_3)$$

where

g = coverage

r = effective reach

ADSTRAT: An Advertising Decision Support System

ESTIMATING MEDIA AID PARAMETERS

- Effective Reach:
    Cross-Tab.

- Probability of Exposure (h_j):
    Starch Scores for Print ad : .4 - .6
    TV (in a Drug Case): .10

- Media Option Source Effect:
    Subjectively.

- Response function $q(y_{st})$:
    Subjectively, based on learning and
    involvement theory.

PROCESS FOR MEDIA SCHEDULING DECISIONS

1. Segment the market and select one or more target audiences.

2. Eliminate certain media and/or vehicles which are obviously inappropriate on qualitative dimensions.

3. Analyze the remaining vehicles based on coverage and cost information and eliminate the least effective alternatives.

4. Schedule ad insertions for remaining vehicles.

Exhibit 7.2

Output from Module:Media:Efficiency
Dataset: media.dat
Parameter file:
Tue Apr 21 22:20:26 1992

ADSTRAT Version 1.0
Copyright 1991, 1992
H. Gatignon & R. Burke

MEDIA EFFICIENCY ANALYSIS

Vehicle Option	Audience Size	Cost/Insertion	Cost/Thousand
CosmopoltnBW	11412	47762	4.19
Cosmopoltn4C	11412	64279	5.63
GoodHskpngBW	20040	90464	4.51
GoodHskpng4C	20040	113509	5.66
LadiesHJrnBW	15154	72270	4.77
LadiesHJrn4C	15154	86020	5.68
McCallsBW	14506	71918	4.96
McCalls4C	14506	84854	5.85
ParentsBW	6441	39369	6.11
Parents4C	6441	50402	7.83
RedbookBW	10505	54841	5.22
Redbook4C	10505	72518	6.90
SeventeenBW	3279	26703	8.14
Seventeen4C	3279	38693	11.80
TrueStoryBW	3791	14113	3.72
TrueStory4C	3791	18343	4.84
WomansDayBW	14618	34150	2.34
WomansDay4C	14618	80383	5.50
WomansWldBW	5942	15180	2.55
WomansWld4C	5942	18150	3.05
BetHomGdnsBW	22535	108257	4.80
BetHomGdns4C	22535	130900	5.81
CountryHomBW	2731	31570	11.56
CountryHom4C	2731	45100	16.51
CountryLivBW	6774	38297	5.65
CountryLiv4C	6774	52399	7.74
FamHndymanBW	3450	23320	6.76
FamHndyman4C	3450	33814	9.80
HomeBW	2378	25383	10.67
Home4C	2378	33820	14.22
HouseBtflBW	3750	31015	8.27
HouseBtfl4C	3750	45535	12.14
MtrpltnHomBW	720	26494	36.80
MtrpltnHom4C	720	36795	51.10
1001HomIdsBW	3471	33539	9.66
1001HomIds4C	3471	40453	11.65
SouthrnLivBW	7096	43637	6.15

SouthrnLiv4C	7096	61534	8.67
SunsetBW	3534	27940	7.91
Sunset4C	3534	38720	10.96
BazaarBW	717	34386	47.96
Bazaar4C	717	33737	47.05
ElleBW	2153	22055	10.24
Elle4C	2153	33083	15.37
GlamourBW	8020	43153	5.38
Glamour4C	8020	60819	7.58
MadmoisellBW	4611	27533	5.97
Madmoisell4C	4611	40018	8.68
VogueBW	5410	28589	5.28
Vogue4C	5410	41162	7.61
PlayboyBW	8519	51271	6.02
Playboy4C	8519	71808	8.43
PenthouseBW	2109	38467	18.24
Penthouse4C	2109	43126	20.45
Field&StrmBW	10837	42510	3.92
Field&Strm4C	10837	63954	5.90
EsquireBW	2638	23925	9.07
Esquire4C	2638	35888	13.60
GQBW	4171	19833	4.75
GQ4C	4171	29788	7.14
BusinessWkBW	6819	38346	5.62
BusinessWk4C	6819	58278	8.55
ForbesBW	3458	30987	8.96
Forbes4C	3458	47102	13.62
FortuneBW	3882	39259	10.11
Fortune4C	3882	60071	15.47
IncBW	1586	31614	19.93
Inc4C	1586	48367	30.50
IndustryWkBW	304	13959	45.92
IndustryWk4C	304	18843	61.98
NatsBsnssBW	866	24585	28.39
NatsBsnss4C	866	36762	42.45
RealEstTodBW	793	17820	22.47
RealEstTod4C	793	22770	28.71
SavvyBW	411	14515	35.32
Savvy4C	411	21703	52.81
JetBW	7964	13184	1.66
Jet4C	7964	18380	2.31
NewsweekBW	18141	69454	3.83
Newsweek4C	18141	111078	6.12
PeopleBW	29751	71225	2.39
People4C	29751	91806	3.09
SportsIllBW	20690	80581	3.89
SportsIll4C	20690	124542	6.02
SportngNwsBW	3758	17072	4.54
SportngNws4C	3758	21505	5.72
TimeBW	21607	84711	3.92

Time4C	21607	132143	6.12
TVGuideBW	39734	105490	2.65
TVGuide4C	39734	124190	3.13
UsBW	4738	24849	5.24
Us4C	4738	32076	6.77
USNws&WldBW	12345	46365	3.76
USNws&Wld4C	12345	69196	5.61
ChngngTimeBW	2098	22259	10.61
ChngngTime4C	2098	31631	15.08
LifeBW	11802	51876	4.40
Life4C	11802	68684	5.82
ModMaturtyBW	20530	203511	9.91
ModMaturty4C	20530	225500	10.98
MoneyBW	6050	48373	8.00
Money4C	6050	75361	12.46
NatlEnqBW	19709	41173	2.09
NatlEnq4C	19709	51920	2.63
NatlGeogrBW	23217	117854	5.08
NatlGeogr4C	23217	153208	6.60
ReadersDigBW	35893	114092	3.18
ReadersDig4C	35893	137203	3.82
SmithsnianBW	6076	37087	6.10
Smithsnian4C	6076	55627	9.16
TheStarBW	11515	31081	2.70
TheStar4C	11515	38346	3.33
YankeeBW	1830	16005	8.75
Yankee4C	1830	21384	11.69
BoysLifeBW	1453	16676	11.48
BoysLife4C	1453	21731	14.96
CareersBW	610	13079	21.44
Careers4C	610	18315	30.02
FastTimesBW	587	15950	27.17
FastTimes4C	587	22550	38.42
JrScholastBW	723	9790	13.54
JrScholast4C	723	44550	61.62
SesameStBW	1228	36453	29.68
SesameSt4C	1228	37730	30.72
NYDailyNews	1242	27715	22.31
LATimes	1130	59030	52.24
NewYorkTimes	1128	49619	43.99
NewYorkPost	540	22253	41.21
PhilaInqrNws	745	41412	55.59
WashPost	781	43022	55.09
ChicagoTrib	747	38669	51.77
SanFranChron	562	37320	66.41
DetroitNews	1318	55697	42.26
NatnlDaytmTV	10989	18893	1.72
NatEarlyNsTV	26277	53543	2.04
NatPrimeTmTV	18977	124273	6.55
NatLateEveTV	6646	23898	3.60

NatWkndKidTV	4128	20020	4.85
CosbyShowTV	36936	412500	11.17
FamilyTiesTV	16105	330000	20.49
CheersTV	27449	247500	9.02
MoonlghtngTV	17464	228250	13.07
WhosTheBssTV	24128	240900	9.98
NightCourtTV	13548	228250	16.85
GrowingPnsTV	16894	217250	12.86
MiamiViceTV	14451	185900	12.86
DynastyTV	19265	203500	10.56
GoldenGrlsTV	28659	192500	6.72
SuperBowlTV	46593	852500	18.30
NewYorkTV	3327	6820	2.05
LsAnglsTV	2164	5610	2.59
ChicagoTV	1759	5885	3.35
PhilaTV	1474	4400	2.99
SanFranTV	1014	3638	3.59
BostonTV	1089	4628	4.25
DetroitTV	978	4071	4.16
DallasTV	926	2915	3.15
WashingTV	871	2585	2.97
HoustonTV	785	3493	4.45
ClvlndTV	830	3850	4.64
AtlantaTV	709	3507	4.95
MinnStPTV	660	1980	3.00
TampStPTV	669	2319	3.47
SttlTacTV	604	1925	3.19
MiamiTV	558	2259	4.05
PittbrgTV	754	2794	3.71
StLouisTV	599	2585	4.32
DenverTV	597	1552	2.60
SacrmntTV	630	2695	4.28

Output from Module:Media:Allocation
Dataset: media.dat
Parameter file:
Tue Apr 21 22:23:26 1992

ADSTRAT Version 1.0
Copyright 1991, 1992
H. Gatignon & R. Burke

MEDIA ALLOCATION

Media name	No. ins	Boundaries min	max	Cost	Effective exposure [000]	Overall vehicle effect	Exp. prob.	Eff. Rch.	Option effect
CosmopoltnBW	0	0	12	0	0	1.00	1.00	1.00	1.00
Cosmopoltn4C	0	0	12	0	0	1.00	1.00	1.00	1.00
GoodHskpngBW	0	0	12	0	0	1.00	1.00	1.00	1.00
GoodHskpng4C	0	0	12	0	0	1.00	1.00	1.00	1.00
LadiesHJrnBW	0	0	12	0	0	1.00	1.00	1.00	1.00
LadiesHJrn4C	0	0	12	0	0	1.00	1.00	1.00	1.00
McCallsBW	0	0	12	0	0	1.00	1.00	1.00	1.00
McCalls4C	0	0	12	0	0	1.00	1.00	1.00	1.00
ParentsBW	0	0	12	0	0	1.00	1.00	1.00	1.00
Parents4C	0	0	12	0	0	1.00	1.00	1.00	1.00
RedbookBW	0	0	12	0	0	1.00	1.00	1.00	1.00
Redbook4C	0	0	12	0	0	1.00	1.00	1.00	1.00
SeventeenBW	0	0	12	0	0	1.00	1.00	1.00	1.00
Seventeen4C	0	0	12	0	0	1.00	1.00	1.00	1.00
TrueStoryBW	0	0	12	0	0	1.00	1.00	1.00	1.00
TrueStory4C	0	0	12	0	0	1.00	1.00	1.00	1.00
WomansDayBW	12	0	12	409800	175416	1.00	1.00	1.00	1.00
WomansDay4C	0	0	12	0	0	1.00	1.00	1.00	1.00
WomansWldBW	12	0	12	182160	71304	1.00	1.00	1.00	1.00
WomansWld4C	12	0	12	217800	71304	1.00	1.00	1.00	1.00
BetHomGdnsBW	0	0	12	0	0	1.00	1.00	1.00	1.00
BetHomGdns4C	0	0	12	0	0	1.00	1.00	1.00	1.00
CountryHomBW	0	0	12	0	0	1.00	1.00	1.00	1.00
CountryHom4C	0	0	12	0	0	1.00	1.00	1.00	1.00
CountryLivBW	0	0	12	0	0	1.00	1.00	1.00	1.00
CountryLiv4C	0	0	12	0	0	1.00	1.00	1.00	1.00
FamHndymanBW	0	0	12	0	0	1.00	1.00	1.00	1.00
FamHndyman4C	0	0	12	0	0	1.00	1.00	1.00	1.00
HomeBW	0	0	12	0	0	1.00	1.00	1.00	1.00
Home4C	0	0	12	0	0	1.00	1.00	1.00	1.00
HouseBtflBW	0	0	12	0	0	1.00	1.00	1.00	1.00
HouseBtfl4C	0	0	12	0	0	1.00	1.00	1.00	1.00
MtrpltnHomBW	0	0	12	0	0	1.00	1.00	1.00	1.00
MtrpltnHom4C	0	0	12	0	0	1.00	1.00	1.00	1.00
1001HomIdsBW	0	0	12	0	0	1.00	1.00	1.00	1.00
1001HomIds4C	0	0	12	0	0	1.00	1.00	1.00	1.00
SouthrnLivBW	0	0	12	0	0	1.00	1.00	1.00	1.00
SouthrnLiv4C	0	0	12	0	0	1.00	1.00	1.00	1.00
SunsetBW	0	0	12	0	0	1.00	1.00	1.00	1.00
Sunset4C	0	0	12	0	0	1.00	1.00	1.00	1.00
BazaarBW	0	0	12	0	0	1.00	1.00	1.00	1.00
Bazaar4C	0	0	12	0	0	1.00	1.00	1.00	1.00
ElleBW	0	0	12	0	0	1.00	1.00	1.00	1.00
Elle4C	0	0	12	0	0	1.00	1.00	1.00	1.00
GlamourBW	0	0	12	0	0	1.00	1.00	1.00	1.00
Glamour4C	0	0	12	0	0	1.00	1.00	1.00	1.00
MadmoisellBW	0	0	12	0	0	1.00	1.00	1.00	1.00
Madmoisell4C	0	0	12	0	0	1.00	1.00	1.00	1.00
VogueBW	0	0	12	0	0	1.00	1.00	1.00	1.00
Vogue4C	0	0	12	0	0	1.00	1.00	1.00	1.00
PlayboyBW	0	0	12	0	0	1.00	1.00	1.00	1.00
Playboy4C	0	0	12	0	0	1.00	1.00	1.00	1.00

PenthouseBW	0	0	12	0	0	1.00	1.00	1.00	1.00
Penthouse4C	0	0	12	0	0	1.00	1.00	1.00	1.00
Field&StrmBW	0	0	12	0	0	1.00	1.00	1.00	1.00
Field&Strm4C	0	0	12	0	0	1.00	1.00	1.00	1.00
EsquireBW	0	0	12	0	0	1.00	1.00	1.00	1.00
Esquire4C	0	0	12	0	0	1.00	1.00	1.00	1.00
GQBW	0	0	12	0	0	1.00	1.00	1.00	1.00
GQ4C	0	0	12	0	0	1.00	1.00	1.00	1.00
BusinessWkBW	0	0	12	0	0	1.00	1.00	1.00	1.00
BusinessWk4C	0	0	12	0	0	1.00	1.00	1.00	1.00
ForbesBW	0	0	12	0	0	1.00	1.00	1.00	1.00
Forbes4C	0	0	12	0	0	1.00	1.00	1.00	1.00
FortuneBW	0	0	12	0	0	1.00	1.00	1.00	1.00
Fortune4C	0	0	12	0	0	1.00	1.00	1.00	1.00
IncBW	0	0	12	0	0	1.00	1.00	1.00	1.00
Inc4C	0	0	12	0	0	1.00	1.00	1.00	1.00
IndustryWkBW	0	0	12	0	0	1.00	1.00	1.00	1.00
IndustryWk4C	0	0	12	0	0	1.00	1.00	1.00	1.00
NatsBsnssBW	0	0	12	0	0	1.00	1.00	1.00	1.00
NatsBsnss4C	0	0	12	0	0	1.00	1.00	1.00	1.00
RealEstTodBW	0	0	12	0	0	1.00	1.00	1.00	1.00
RealEstTod4C	0	0	12	0	0	1.00	1.00	1.00	1.00
SavvyBW	0	0	12	0	0	1.00	1.00	1.00	1.00
Savvy4C	0	0	12	0	0	1.00	1.00	1.00	1.00
JetBW	12	0	12	158208	95568	1.00	1.00	1.00	1.00
Jet4C	12	0	12	220560	95568	1.00	1.00	1.00	1.00
NewsweekBW	0	0	12	0	0	1.00	1.00	1.00	1.00
Newsweek4C	0	0	12	0	0	1.00	1.00	1.00	1.00
PeopleBW	12	0	12	854700	357012	1.00	1.00	1.00	1.00
People4C	0	0	12	0	0	1.00	1.00	1.00	1.00
SportsIllBW	0	0	12	0	0	1.00	1.00	1.00	1.00
SportsIll4C	0	0	12	0	0	1.00	1.00	1.00	1.00
SportngNwsBW	0	0	12	0	0	1.00	1.00	1.00	1.00
SportngNws4C	0	0	12	0	0	1.00	1.00	1.00	1.00
TimeBW	0	0	12	0	0	1.00	1.00	1.00	1.00
Time4C	0	0	12	0	0	1.00	1.00	1.00	1.00
TVGuideBW	12	0	12	1265880	476808	1.00	1.00	1.00	1.00
TVGuide4C	0	0	12	0	0	1.00	1.00	1.00	1.00
UsBW	0	0	12	0	0	1.00	1.00	1.00	1.00
Us4C	0	0	12	0	0	1.00	1.00	1.00	1.00
USNws&WldBW	0	0	12	0	0	1.00	1.00	1.00	1.00
USNws&Wld4C	0	0	12	0	0	1.00	1.00	1.00	1.00
ChngngTimeBW	0	0	12	0	0	1.00	1.00	1.00	1.00
ChngngTime4C	0	0	12	0	0	1.00	1.00	1.00	1.00
LifeBW	0	0	12	0	0	1.00	1.00	1.00	1.00
Life4C	0	0	12	0	0	1.00	1.00	1.00	1.00
ModMaturtyBW	0	0	12	0	0	1.00	1.00	1.00	1.00
ModMaturty4C	0	0	12	0	0	1.00	1.00	1.00	1.00
MoneyBW	0	0	12	0	0	1.00	1.00	1.00	1.00
Money4C	0	0	12	0	0	1.00	1.00	1.00	1.00
NatlEnqBW	12	0	12	494076	236508	1.00	1.00	1.00	1.00
NatlEnq4C	12	0	12	623040	236508	1.00	1.00	1.00	1.00
NatlGeogrBW	0	0	12	0	0	1.00	1.00	1.00	1.00
NatlGeogr4C	0	0	12	0	0	1.00	1.00	1.00	1.00
ReadersDigBW	0	0	12	0	0	1.00	1.00	1.00	1.00
ReadersDig4C	0	0	12	0	0	1.00	1.00	1.00	1.00
SmithsnianBW	0	0	12	0	0	1.00	1.00	1.00	1.00
Smithsnian4C	0	0	12	0	0	1.00	1.00	1.00	1.00
TheStarBW	12	0	12	372972	138180	1.00	1.00	1.00	1.00
TheStar4C	0	0	12	0	0	1.00	1.00	1.00	1.00
YankeeBW	0	0	12	0	0	1.00	1.00	1.00	1.00
Yankee4C	0	0	12	0	0	1.00	1.00	1.00	1.00

BoysLifeBW	0	0	12	0	0	1.00	1.00	1.00	1.00
BoysLife4C	0	0	12	0	0	1.00	1.00	1.00	1.00
CareersBW	0	0	12	0	0	1.00	1.00	1.00	1.00
Careers4C	0	0	12	0	0	1.00	1.00	1.00	1.00
FastTimesBW	0	0	12	0	0	1.00	1.00	1.00	1.00
FastTimes4C	0	0	12	0	0	1.00	1.00	1.00	1.00
JrScholastBW	0	0	12	0	0	1.00	1.00	1.00	1.00
JrScholast4C	0	0	12	0	0	1.00	1.00	1.00	1.00
SesameStBW	0	0	12	0	0	1.00	1.00	1.00	1.00
SesameSt4C	0	0	12	0	0	1.00	1.00	1.00	1.00
NYDailyNews	0	0	12	0	0	1.00	1.00	1.00	1.00
LATimes	0	0	12	0	0	1.00	1.00	1.00	1.00
NewYorkTimes	0	0	12	0	0	1.00	1.00	1.00	1.00
NewYorkPost	0	0	12	0	0	1.00	1.00	1.00	1.00
PhilaInqrNws	0	0	12	0	0	1.00	1.00	1.00	1.00
WashPost	0	0	12	0	0	1.00	1.00	1.00	1.00
ChicagoTrib	0	0	12	0	0	1.00	1.00	1.00	1.00
SanFranChron	0	0	12	0	0	1.00	1.00	1.00	1.00
DetroitNews	0	0	12	0	0	1.00	1.00	1.00	1.00
NatnlDaytmTV	12	0	12	226716	131868	1.00	1.00	1.00	1.00
NatEarlyNsTV	12	0	12	642516	315324	1.00	1.00	1.00	1.00
NatPrimeTmTV	0	0	12	0	0	1.00	1.00	1.00	1.00
NatLateEveTV	0	0	12	0	0	1.00	1.00	1.00	1.00
NatWkndKidTV	0	0	12	0	0	1.00	1.00	1.00	1.00
CosbyShowTV	0	0	12	0	0	1.00	1.00	1.00	1.00
FamilyTiesTV	0	0	12	0	0	1.00	1.00	1.00	1.00
CheersTV	0	0	12	0	0	1.00	1.00	1.00	1.00
MoonlghtngTV	0	0	12	0	0	1.00	1.00	1.00	1.00
WhosTheBssTV	0	0	12	0	0	1.00	1.00	1.00	1.00
NightCourtTV	0	0	12	0	0	1.00	1.00	1.00	1.00
GrowingPnsTV	0	0	12	0	0	1.00	1.00	1.00	1.00
MiamiViceTV	0	0	12	0	0	1.00	1.00	1.00	1.00
DynastyTV	0	0	12	0	0	1.00	1.00	1.00	1.00
GoldenGrlsTV	0	0	12	0	0	1.00	1.00	1.00	1.00
SuperBowlTV	0	0	12	0	0	1.00	1.00	1.00	1.00
NewYorkTV	12	0	12	81840	39924	1.00	1.00	1.00	1.00
LsAnglsTV	12	0	12	67320	25968	1.00	1.00	1.00	1.00
ChicagoTV	0	0	12	0	0	1.00	1.00	1.00	1.00
PhilaTV	12	0	12	52800	17688	1.00	1.00	1.00	1.00
SanFranTV	0	0	12	0	0	1.00	1.00	1.00	1.00
BostonTV	0	0	12	0	0	1.00	1.00	1.00	1.00
DetroitTV	0	0	12	0	0	1.00	1.00	1.00	1.00
DallasTV	12	0	12	34980	11112	1.00	1.00	1.00	1.00
WashingTV	12	0	12	31020	10452	1.00	1.00	1.00	1.00
HoustonTV	0	0	12	0	0	1.00	1.00	1.00	1.00
ClvlndTV	0	0	12	0	0	1.00	1.00	1.00	1.00
AtlantaTV	0	0	12	0	0	1.00	1.00	1.00	1.00
MinnStPTV	12	0	12	23760	7920	1.00	1.00	1.00	1.00
TampStPTV	0	0	12	0	0	1.00	1.00	1.00	1.00
SttlTacTV	11	0	12	21175	6644	1.00	1.00	1.00	1.00
MiamiTV	0	0	12	0	0	1.00	1.00	1.00	1.00
PittbrgTV	0	0	12	0	0	1.00	1.00	1.00	1.00
StLouisTV	0	0	12	0	0	1.00	1.00	1.00	1.00
DenverTV	12	0	12	18624	7164	1.00	1.00	1.00	1.00
SacrmntTV	0	0	12	0	0	1.00	1.00	1.00	1.00

```
Total used: 5999947  of budget: 6000000
100.0% of budget used
2528240 total effective exposure
```

Exhibit 7.4

Output from Module:Situation:Tabulate
Dataset: survey.dat,factor.dat,cluster.dat

Mon Jun 22 11:21:52 1992

ADSTRAT Version 1.0
Copyright 1991, 1992
H. Gatignon & R. Burke

CROSS TABULATION

Cluster		ReadFashion 0	1
1	Freq	10	55
	Perct	3.33	18.33
	Row %	15.38	84.62
	Col %	10.53	26.83
2	Freq	0	33
	Perct	0.00	11.00
	Row %	0.00	100.00
	Col %	0.00	16.10
3	Freq	49	47
	Perct	16.33	15.67
	Row %	51.04	48.96
	Col %	51.58	22.93
4	Freq	23	30
	Perct	7.67	10.00
	Row %	43.40	56.60
	Col %	24.21	14.63
5	Freq	13	40
	Perct	4.33	13.33
	Row %	24.53	75.47
	Col %	13.68	19.51

Chi Square =   44.528
Degree of freedom =   4

Exhibit 7.5

Output from Module:Situation:Tabulate
Dataset: survey.dat,factor.dat,cluster.dat

Mon Jun 22 11:22:35 1992

ADSTRAT Version 1.0
Copyright 1991, 1992
H. Gatignon & R. Burke

CROSS TABULATION

Cluster		WtchDayTV 0	1
1	Freq	55	10
	Perct	18.33	3.33
	Row %	84.62	15.38
	Col %	22.09	19.61
2	Freq	29	4
	Perct	9.67	1.33
	Row %	87.88	12.12
	Col %	11.65	7.84
3	Freq	76	20
	Perct	25.33	6.67
	Row %	79.17	20.83
	Col %	30.52	39.22
4	Freq	45	8
	Perct	15.00	2.67
	Row %	84.91	15.09
	Col %	18.07	15.69
5	Freq	44	9
	Perct	14.67	3.00
	Row %	83.02	16.98
	Col %	17.67	17.65

Chi Square =   1.813
Degree of freedom =   4

Exhibit 7.6

Output from Module:Media:Allocation
Dataset: media.dat
Parameter file:
Fri Apr 24 13:41:50 1992

ADSTRAT Version 1.0
Copyright 1991, 1992
H. Gatignon & R. Burke

MEDIA ALLOCATION

Media name	No. ins	Boundaries min	max	Cost	Effective exposure [000]	Overall vehicle effect	Exp. prob.	Eff. Rch.	Option effect
WomansDayBW	0	0	12	0	0	0.05	0.50	0.10	1.00
WomansWldBW	0	0	12	0	0	0.05	0.50	0.10	1.00
WomansWld4C	0	0	12	0	0	0.10	1.00	0.10	1.00
Glamour4C	1	0	12	60819	2165	0.27	1.00	0.27	1.00
JetBW	12	0	12	158208	9557	0.10	0.50	0.20	1.00
Jet4C	12	0	12	220560	19114	0.20	1.00	0.20	1.00
PeopleBW	12	0	12	854700	35701	0.10	0.50	0.20	1.00
TVGuideBW	12	0	12	1265880	66753	0.14	0.70	0.20	1.00
NatlEnqBW	12	0	12	494076	18921	0.08	0.50	0.16	1.00
NatlEnq4C	12	0	12	623040	37841	0.16	1.00	0.16	1.00
TheStarBW	0	0	12	0	0	0.08	0.50	0.16	1.00
NatnlDaytmTV	0	0	12	0	0	0.04	0.20	0.20	1.00
NatEarlyNsTV	0	0	12	0	0	0.06	0.30	0.20	1.00
MoonlghtngTV	0	0	12	0	0	0.26	1.00	0.26	1.00
MiamiViceTV	0	0	12	0	0	0.29	1.00	0.29	1.00
DynastyTV	0	0	12	0	0	0.29	1.00	0.29	1.00
GoldenGrlsTV	12	0	12	2310000	92855	0.27	1.00	0.27	1.00

Total used: 5987283   of budget: 6000000
99.8% of budget used
282907 total effective exposure

Exhibit 7.7

MEDIA AID

Budget (enter dollar amount):6000000.00

Number of Time Periods (1 to 12):12

Number of Segments (1 to 5): 1

Number of Media (1 to 10): 8

Enter Percentage of Potential Realized (in percent. e.g. 60)

```
              at saturation: 100
              at 0 exposures:   0
     at 1 average exposure:    30
     at 3 average exposures:   80
```

Population (Number of Consumers) and
Potential (Average Dollar Sales per Consumer) in each Segment
Segment   1   2   3   4   5

Population: 295000.00:_____:_____:_____:_____
Potential :   340.00:_____:_____:_____:_____

Memory Constant (e.g. 0.75):0.75

Exposure Values (Source Effect) and
Probability of Exposure (Probability of seeing ad in vehicle)
Media   1   2   3   4   5   6   7   8   9   10

Exposure
Value   :1.00:1.00:1.00:1.00:1.00:1.00:1.00:1.00:____:____

Exposure
Prob.   :1.00:0.50:1.00:0.50:0.70:0.50:1.00:1.00:____:____

Effective reach
(Percentage of Audience that belongs to Segment, e.g. 16.0)
Segments 1   2   3   4   5
Media
    1   :27.00:_____:_____:_____:_____
    2   :20.00:_____:_____:_____:_____
    3   :20.00:_____:_____:_____:_____
    4   :20.00:_____:_____:_____:_____
    5   :20.00:_____:_____:_____:_____
    6   :16.00:_____:_____:_____:_____
    7   :16.00:_____:_____:_____:_____
    8   :27.00:_____:_____:_____:_____
    9   :_____:_____:_____:_____:_____
   10   :_____:_____:_____:_____:_____

Media #	Average Cost Per Insertion Cost (in dollars)	Maximum Insertions per period	Audience size
1	:60819.00	: 1	:8020000.0
2	:13184.00	: 4	:7964000.0
3	:18380.00	: 4	:7964000.0
4	:71225.00	: 4	:29751000.
5	:105490.0	: 4	: 39734.00
6	:41173.00	: 4	:19709000.
7	:51920.00	: 4	:19709000.
8	:192500.0	: 4	:28659000.
9	:_____	:____	:_____
10	:_____	:____	:_____

Exhibit 7.8

Output from Module:Media:MediaAid
Dataset: None
Parameter file:
Fri Apr 24 16:23:05 1992

ADSTRAT Version 1.0
Copyright 1991, 1992
H. Gatignon & R. Burke

MEDIA AID

Sales per segment

Period	Segments 1	Total Sales	Expenses
1	100296859.03	100296859.03	1614347.00
2	100298025.45	100298025.45	701182.00
3	100298428.80	100298428.80	618836.00
4	100298407.35	100298407.35	405161.00
5	100298390.97	100298390.97	405161.00
6	100298378.52	100298378.52	405161.00
7	100298369.09	100298369.09	405161.00
8	100298259.56	100298259.56	333936.00
9	100298170.04	100298170.04	333936.00
10	100298098.32	100298098.32	333936.00
11	100298041.74	100298041.74	333936.00
12	100297059.11	100297059.11	73520.00

Total Overall Sales:1203576487.97

Ratio Cost/Budget: 0.994046

Optimal MEDIA AID Schedule

Media--Time	1	2	3	4	5	6	7	8	9	10	11	12
1	1	0	0	0	0	0	0	0	0	0	0	0
2	4	4	4	4	4	4	4	4	4	4	4	0
3	4	4	4	4	4	4	4	4	4	4	4	4
4	4	4	4	1	1	1	1	0	0	0	0	0
5	0	0	0	0	0	0	0	0	0	0	0	0
6	4	2	0	0	0	0	0	0	0	0	0	0
7	4	4	4	4	4	4	4	4	4	4	0	0
8	4	0	0	0	0	0	0	0	0	0	0	0

8

Copy Decisions

At least two class sessions are needed to discuss copy issues. The first session covers advertising creative strategy and the design of ad execution. This is the creative work of the advertising agency. This session can be extended to include a discussion of consumer behavior theories relevant to copy decisions. These issues are addressed in the expert system provided with ADSTRAT, which is an adaptation of the ADCAD system. It should be noted that the expert system's knowledge base covers a broad range of consumer products and services, and can be applied to situations other than the ADSTRAT data sets. Exhibit 8.2 presents an example consultion for brand SONO and the Singles segment, and identifies sources of information for user input. The second class session covers issues of copy testing.

SESSION 1

The first session is divided into three parts, which describe: (1) who is involved in the copy decision, (2) tools that facilitate the creative process, and (3) what copy works when.

1. *Who is involved in the copy decision?*

   This discussion provides an opportunity for the instructor to describe to the students how the advertising agency is organized.

2. *Tools that facilitate the creative process.*

   ■ *Psychographic segmentation.* This topic was discussed when we introduced the target selection decision. Although the students should be familiar with psychographics by now, it is important to discuss how a psychographic profile of the target market can be used to help design ad executions. The ad copy can be tailored to describe or represent consumers that resemble the target audience. This is especially important with transformational advertisements, where consumers in the audience must imagine the experience of using the product and see themselves in that situation.

■ *Studies based on past experience.* The purpose of this discussion is to explain how advertising research is used for copy design. Students often raise the concern that research may constrain advertising creativity. It is therefore important to discuss how research can be a constructive guide to the creative process. The quotes by David Ogilvy included in the transparencies can be a useful vehicle to convince students that research is important for copy decisions.

■ *Techniques for enhancing creativity.* This discussion is particularly useful when students are asked to develop advertising copy as part of the ADSTRAT assignment. A transparency in Exhibit 8.1 lists various methods for generating new creative concepts.

3. *What copy works when?*

This section is divided into two parts: the copy format (e.g., ad size, color, position) and the execution strategy and characteristics. The transparencies provided in Exhibit 8.1 cover the main issues, although each could certainly be developed further.

SESSION 2

The session on copy testing is relatively straightforward. The objective of the session is to show that advertising copy selection involves considerable research at various stages in the copy development process. We review the various types of copy research methods, and discuss criteria for evaluating commercial copy testing services. Finally, we present students with descriptions of these commercial services (see the transparencies at the end of Exhibit 8.1).

Exhibit 8.1

Transparencies
for
Copy Decisions

COPY DECISIONS
Session 1

CREATIVE PROCESS

1. Who is involved?

2. What are tools to facilitate the creative process?

3. Copy execution: what works when?

1. WHO IS INVOLVED?

Ad Agency

- artists
- creative director
- agency research department
- account executives

Advertiser
- brand management
- marketing research
- top executives

2. WHAT ARE THE TOOLS THAT CAN FACILITATE THE CREATIVE PROCESS?

- Psychographic segmentation

- Research based on past experience

- Techniques for enhancing creativity

PSYCHOGRAPHIC SEGMENTATION

RESEARCH BASED ON PAST EXPERIENCE

- The purpose of research is to find rules about what works and what does not work when.

- David Ogilvy responds to criticisms of a research orientation.

1.   "The creative process can't be reduced
to a set of rules."

We're not imposing rules, but reporting how most
consumers react, most of the time, to different
stimuli.

2.   "The best advertising arises from the creative person's instinct and intuition, not from formulae."

We are at pains to tell our creative colleagues that, while knowledge of positive and negative factors will help them avoid egregious mistakes, it is no substitute for the invention of Big Ideas. And these are the products of the unconscious.

3. "Some of the most successful campaigns go against the average."

This is true. But it leads to a fault in reasoning—the doctrine that, since some people succeed by going against the averages, the best way to succeed is to go against them. A blind pig may sometimes find truffles, but it helps if he forages in an oak forest.

4.   "Adherence to averages never will result
      in outstanding work."

This isn't true. Many successful ad campaigns come
from inspired use of tried-and-true techniques.
Above-average techniques don't condemn you to
mediocre results. Nor will they guarantee success.
But they do improve the chances that you won't
waste money.

TECHNIQUES FOR ENHANCING CREATIVITY

- Brainstorming

- Synectics

- Free association

- Challenge your assumptions by asking "what if..."

- Come up with ideas first and then ask "why not?"

- Avoid competitors' executions

COPY EXECUTION: WHAT WORKS WHEN?

"It is not uncommon for a change in headline to multiply returns from five to ten times over."

Claude Hopkins

COPY EXECUTION: WHAT WORKS WHEN?

"I have seen one advertisement actually sell not twice as much, not three times as much, but 19 1/2 times as much as another. Both advertisements occupied the same space. Both were run in the same publication. Both had photographic illustrations. Both had carefully written copy. The difference was that one used the right appeal and the other used the wrong appeal."

David Ogilvy

COPY EXECUTION: WHAT WORKS WHEN?

1.   Format Characteristics

2.   Execution Strategy

ADSTRAT: An Advertising Decision Support System

1. FORMAT CHARACTERISTICS

- Size of ad
- Position of ad
- Color
- Intensity
- Novelty
- Contrast
- Variation

1. FORMAT CHARACTERISTICS

Prediction of Readership
(% who remember reading or seeing any part of ad)

	weights
1. Size of ad	.441
2. Number of colors	.341
3. Square inches of illustration	.285

ADSTRAT: An Advertising Decision Support System

1. FORMAT CHARACTERISTICS

Industrial Products

	Routine Products	Unique Products	Important Products
Recall/readership			
Photographs	+		
Illustration	+		
Women	+	+	
Ad Size		+	+
Pointers		+	
Color			+
Multiple Products			-
Inquiry			
Ad Size	+		+
Color		+	+
Multiple Products	+		
Pointers	+		
Free Offers		+	

EXECUTION STRATEGY

A.   Type of appeal

B.   Inclusions and Omissions

C.   Order of Presentation

D.   Use of Presenter

E.   Informational vs. Transformational

A. TYPE OF APPEAL

- Fear Appeal

- Humor

- Sex Appeal

B. INCLUSIONS AND OMISSIONS

- Multiproposition vs. USP (Complexity)

- Implicit vs. Explicit

- Message Arguments (Sidedness & Comparative)

ADSTRAT: An Advertising Decision Support System

ADSTRAT: An Advertising Decision Support System

C. ORDER OF PRESENTATION

- Message Order

D. USE OF PRESENTER

Presenter Characteristics

- Recognition
- Attractiveness
- Similarity
- Expertise
- Trustworthiness
- Company Affiliation

D. USE OF PRESENTER

Source Credibility

Predisposition	Most Effective	Reasons
-	Hi Cred.	Counter arg.
+	Lo Cred.	Support arg.
0	+	

E. INFORMATIONAL VS. TRANSFORMATIONAL

Informational   *Transformational*

- Problem-solution
- One or two benefits

- Emotional authenticity
- Unique emotion execution
- Ad must be liked
- Implicit benefit delivery

COPY DECISIONS
Session 2:

COPY TESTING

COPY TESTING ISSUES

1. **How should the test be conducted?**
    - Natural setting vs. forced exposure
    - Single vs. multiple exposures

2. **What criteria should be used to evaluate an ad?**
    - Day-after-recall
    - Persuasion testing
    - Behavior monitoring

3. **How do we evaluate copy testing methods?**

1. HOW SHOULD THE TEST BE CONDUCTED?

Stages for Tests

STAGE 1:   Positioning/Message strategy

STAGE 2:   Early creative process

STAGE 3:   Copy execution available

Stages for Tests

STAGE 1: Positioning/Message strategy

No testing

Strategies deduced from positioning and segmentation studies

Stages for Tests

STAGE 2: Early creative process

Objective: Verify whether or not message ideas are interpreted correctly.

Techniques: Projective methods.
- word-association tests
- sentence completion tests
- unstructured interviews (focus groups)

No measure of effect of ad copy

Stages for Tests

STAGE 3: When copy execution is available

Objective: To predict how effective the ad is going to be.

Methods: • Nature of setting
  ○ Laboratory
  ○ Field test
  • Criteria used for evaluation

COPY TESTING METHODS

- Laboratory:
    - ASI
    - ARS
    - Mc Collum/Spielman

- Field tests:
    - Starch
    - Burke
    - Behaviorscan
    - Ad-Tel

COPY TESTING METHODS: CRITERIA
STAGES OF INFORMATION PROCESSING

1. Exposure

2. Attention

3. Comprehension

4. Acceptance

5. Retention

6. Behavior

COPY TESTING METHODS: CRITERIA

1. Recognition measurements (Starch, Burke)

2. Recall (Burke, McCollum Spielman, ARS)

3. Attitude and opinion (ASI, Gallup & Robinson)

4. Comprehension

5. Believability of
    - ad theme
    - proposition
    - facts

6. Persuasion measures

7. Buying predisposition

COPY TESTING METHODS: CRITERIA (continued)

8. Ad preference ratings
    - Paired comparisons of preferences for ads
    - Order of merit tests

9. Behavioral measures
    - simulated purchase (ASI, ARS)
    - product choice (Ad-tel, Behaviorscan, ScanAmerica)

10. Physiological Measures
    - Heart rate
    - Pupil dilation
    - GSR
    - EEG
    - Facial EMG

3. HOW DO WE EVALUATE COPY TESTING METHODS?

- Validity

- Reliability

- Repetition of exposures

- Time effects

- Interaction

- Diagnostic

OPTIMAL NUMBER OF AD EXECUTIONS TO TEST

Is there a magic number?

Between 3 and 6.

COPY TESTING SERVICES

☞ STARCH
- 15-30 urban locations
- Door-to-door interviewing
- Recognition scores for magazine readers
  - noted readers (% of readers who remembered that they had seen the ad in the particular issue)
  - associated readers (% of readers who have seen or read any part of the ad that clearly indicated the brand or advertiser)
  - read most (% of readers who read 50% or more of written material)
- Competitive information: 85-90 ads per magazine
- Sample: 200-300 (1/2 males, 1/2 females)
- Cost: very cheap (around $500)

ADSTRAT: An Advertising Decision Support System

COPY TESTING SERVICES

☞ BURKE: DAY-AFTER RECALL
- 1 to 4 locations
- Telephone interview day after viewing
- Question sequence:
  ○ Check that respondent is in target audience (8/100)
  ○ Check that respondent is a program viewer
  ○ Check that respondent viewed commercial (claimed recall)
  ○ Three sets of questions:
    · Do you remember seeing a commercial for a *laundry detergent*?
    · Do you remember seeing a commercial for *Tide laundry detergent*?
    (if yes to either of the above)
    · What did the commercial say about the product? What did the commercial show? What did the commercial look like? What ideas were brought out? (recorded verbatim)
- Sample: 150
- Cost: Cheap (around $6000 + media time)

COPY TESTING SERVICES

☞ AD-TEL
- 3 locations
- Matched panels of homes
  - 2 or 3 panels per city
  - different degrees of matching in different cities
- Controlled advertising
  - Representative sample of the target
  - Natural exposure
  - No control of sales caused by something else
  - Sensitive
  - Reliable
  - Fast
- Cost: Moderate (around $100,000 for six months in one market + around $30,000 for analysis)

COPY TESTING SERVICES

☞ BEHAVIORSCAN
- 2 cities
- Computer-matched panels of homes
  - ◦ many different panels per city
  - ◦ can match on most variables
- UPC Scanner data

COPY TESTING SERVICES

☞ McCOLLUM/SPIELMAN
- 3 locations: East, Middle, West Coast
- Respondents recruited by mail
- Test Sequence:
  - Orientation
  - Classification based on
    - Demographics, and
    - Pre-motivation measures (brand & product usage)
  - TV program I (clutter format)
  - TV program reaction questions
  - Unaided measures:
    - clutter/awareness
    - brand and product recall
    - recall of main idea of copy
  - TV program II (commercials in island positions)
  - TV program questions
  - Post-motivation measures
    - brand selection for shopping bag prize
  - Test commercial diagnostics

COPY TESTING SERVICES

↬ ARS
- 2 locations: Boston & Chicago
- Respondents recruited by mail
- Sequence:
  - Pre-motivation measure (brand preference for prize)
  - Attendance prize
  - Pilot #1 with 3 pairs of commercials
  - Demographic and program questions
  - Pilot #2 with 3 pairs of commercials
  - Post-motivation measure
  - 3 days after recall
- Persuasion measure

$$FS = \text{Fair Share} = \text{Expected pre/post shift}$$
$$SP = \text{Switching portion} = \text{Historical norms of category non-loyals}$$
$$B = \text{\# brands to choose among in pre/post choice}$$
$$PCP = \text{Pre-Choice Portion}$$
$$FS = SP(3/B - PCP)$$
(the 3 was empirically determined)

COPY TESTING SERVICES

- ∞ AUDIENCE STUDIES, INC.
  - Los Angeles
  - Recruiting: shopping center interview + telephone
  - Sequence:
    - ◦ demographics
    - ◦ pre-persuasion measure (brand selection/preference for awards)
    - ◦ Cartoon 1 & Pilot 1 (no commercials)
    - ◦ TV program reaction questions
    - ◦ Clutter of 5 commercials with diagnostic check list after each ad
    - ◦ Group discussion
    - ◦ Pilot 2
    - ◦ Post persuasion
  - Sample size: 250
  - Cost: $4000 (+$1000 extra for focus group)

COPY TESTING SERVICES

☞ GALLUP & ROBINSON
- 10 urban locations
- Test issue placed with 300 regular readers
- Recall questions asked next day
  - ○ proven name recognition
  - ○ sales message registration (idea registration)
  - ○ favorable attitude
- Competitive information: up to 30 ads per magazine

Exhibit 8.2

An Example Consultation with Expert System

The user first enters the name of the brand to be advertised, its product class, the benefit on which the brand will be positioned, and the name of the targeted market segment into the Expert System template. In the following example, we would like to develop advertising for brand SONO which will appeal to the Singles segment. The brand positioning (on the attribute power, in this example) can be derived from the *Positioning* analysis reported in Chapter 5 of this manual. Based on the *Advisor* module's recommendations, we will attempt to stimulate Singles' trial of SONO by communicating a brand image, mood, or lifestyle, and by maintaining top-of-mind brand awareness. This information is entered into the template. The user then checks off communications variables to be determined. In the example shown below, the user has asked the system to recommend possible ad formats, executional techniques, presenter attributes, benefit communication approaches, and emotional appeals.

```
                 EXPERT SYSTEM FOR COPY DECISIONS

Brand Name:SONO                              Product Class:Sonite
Brand Positioning:Power                      Target Audience:Singles

Marketing Objectives
(check all that apply)

        Stimulate primary demand:__
        Reinforce primary demand:__
        Stimulate brand trial:x
        Stimulate repeat purchase or loyalty:__
        Increase rate of brand usage:__
        Attract trier-rejectors:__

Communication Objectives
(check all that apply)

        Create/increase brand recognition:__
        Create/increase top-of-mind brand awareness:__
        Communicate category characteristics:__
        Communicate category image/mood/lifestyle:__
        Communicate brand characteristics:__
        Communicate brand image/mood/lifestyle:x
        Maintain brand recognition:__
        Maintain top-of-mind brand awareness:x
```

```
      Reinforce category beliefs:__
      Reinforce category image/mood/lifestyle:__
      Reinforce positive brand beliefs:__
      Reinforce brand image/mood/lifestyle:__
      Communicate brand changes/enhancements:__
      Communicate new brand image/mood/lifestyle:__
      Communicate new brand uses:__

Select ad characteristics to be determined
(check all that apply)

      Ad format:x
      Executional technique:x
      Presenter attributes:x
      Benefit communication:x
      Emotional appeal:x
```

After the user "Escapes" from edit mode and selects the "Output" option, the system asks a series of questions about the situation. In the following text, each Expert System question is accompanied by a note describing the source of the answer (shown in boldface). The name of the analysis module and associated variables are shown in italics. This example assumes that the user has first run the Describe and Classify options to assign survey respondents to clusters, as described in Chapter 4.

```
The creative strategy of SONO is transformational.

The value is transformational because the ad objective of SONO is communicate
brand image/mood/lifestyle.

  Is this acceptable (y/n)?  y
```

* **ADSTRAT** recommends a transformational creative strategy based on the ad objective selected by the user, and asks for confirmation. This would seem to be appropriate given the sensory nature of the product experience, so the user responds **yes**. If this is not acceptable, the user can override ADSTRAT's recommendation and select an informational creative strategy.

```
What is the visibility in the ad of Power?
Known values are
     1.  low
     2.  high
>> low
```

* Based on general knowledge of electronic products and their distribution outlets, we can assume that Sonites are prominently displayed at the point of purchase.

```
What is the difference between brands perceived by Singles?
Known values are
     1.  small
     2.  medium
     3.  large
>> medium
```

* *Situation:Tabulate* - Most Singles (Cluster 1) perceive the differences between the various brands of Sonites to be small to **medium**). Eighty-nine percent rate *PerceivedDif* between 2 and 5 (on a 1 to 7 scale).

```
What is the brand performance knowledge of Singles?
Known values are
     1.  low
     2.  high
>> high
```

* *Situation:Tabulate* - While there are no survey items which test consumers' knowledge of SONO's performance, Singles do report having **high** knowledge of the Sonite product category (*KnowledgeSon*).

```
The economic decision risk for Singles is low.
The value is low because
   the brand performance knowledge of Singles is high.

Is this acceptable (y/n)?  n
```

* Because we told **ADSTRAT** that Singles have considerable knowledge about SONO's performance, the system concludes that the risk of consumers losing money by selecting an inferior alternative is low. However, based on the high cost of SONO, the complexity of the product, and the infrequency of purchase, we infer that the risk may be high, so we override this conclusion (see below).

```
What is the absolute price of SONO?
Known values are
     1.   inexpensive
     2.   somewhat expensive
     3.   very expensive
>> 3
```

* *Situation:Trend* - The *Price* of SONO in period 8 is $340, which, on an absolute scale, is **very expensive.**

```
What is the economic decision risk for Singles?
Known values are
     1.   low
     2.   high
>> high

The economic decision risk for Singles is high.
The value is high because
  you said so.

Is this acceptable (y/n)?  y
```

* As noted above, we changed ADSTRAT's initial conclusion concerning economic decision risk to **high** in line with our intuition about the product category.

```
The decision involvement of Singles is high.
The value is high because
  the economic decision risk for Singles is high.

Is this acceptable (y/n)?  y
```

* Because the economic decision risk is high, ADSTRAT concludes that this is a high involvement decision for Singles. The user accepts this conclusion.

```
What is the decision making unit of Singles?
Known values are
     1.   individual
     2.   group
>> individual
```

* *Situation:Tabulate)* - Most Singles (54% of Cluster 1) report that they would make the decision about which brand of Sonite to purchase by themselves, rather than with the help of others (*OtherInfinc*). Therefore, we assume that this is an **individual** decision. Since

a large minority (46%) of Singles are influenced by others, the user might want to run ADSTRAT with both input alternatives and compare the differences in recommendations.

```
What is the brand attitude of Singles?
Known values are
     1.   negative
     2.   neutral
     3.   positive
>> positive
```

* Given the relatively high purchase intent of Singles toward brand SONO, we can infer that their brand attitude is positive.

```
The message processing motivation of Singles is high.
The value is high because
   the decision involvement of Singles is high,
   and the decision making unit of Singles is individual,
   and the brand attitude of Singles is positive.

Is this acceptable (y/n)?  y
```

* When consumers are involved in a decision and are making this decision by themselves, they are likely to attend to relevant advertising messages. This is particularly true when they have a positive attitude towards the advertised brand (and are therefore not defensive).

```
What is the product type of SONO?
Known values are
     1.   existing brand
     2.   line extension of an existing brand
     3.   minor modification of an existing brand
     4.   major modification of an existing brand
     5.   new brand
>> 1
```

* *Situation:Trend - UnitSales* of SONO were 75,000 in period 1, and have risen to 348,000 units in period 8. Therefore, SONO would be considered an **existing brand**.

```
What is the average age of Singles?
Known values are
     1.   child
     2.   teen
     3.   adult
     4.   elderly
>> adult
```

* *Situation:Tabulate* - Ninety-two percent of Singles (Cluster 1) are between 18 and 38 years of age.

```
What is the product purchase anxiety of Singles?
Known values are
     1.   low
     2.   high
>> low
```

* The Sonite product is not associated with personal hygiene or other "sensitive" issues. Therefore, consumer purchase anxiety is likely to be **low**.

```
What are the brand purchase motivations of Singles?
Known values are
     1.   problem removal
     2.   problem avoidance
     3.   dissatisfaction with current brand
     4.   sensory stimulation
     5.   intellectual stimulation
     6.   social approval
     7.   self esteem
>> 4,6
```

* *Situation:Tabulate* - Forty percent of Singles (Cluster 1) purchase a particular brand of Sonite *(BrandMotiv)* for **sensory stimulation**, while 50 percent purchase it for **social approval**. A small group purchases the brand for **intellectual stimulation**, but we can neglect this group for purposes of analysis. Brand purchase motivation is a multi-valued variable. Therefore, the user can enter multiple responses, separated by commas.

```
What is the level of complexity of Sonite?
Known values are
     1.  low
     2.  high
>> high
```

* Based on general knowledge of electronics products and the characteristics of Sonites (weight, design, volume, maximum frequency, and power), we might infer that the complexity of Sonites is high.

```
What is the product class knowledge of Singles?
Known values are
     1.  low
     2.  high
>> high
```

* *Situation:Tabulate* - As noted earlier, Singles report having **high** knowledge of the Sonite product category (*KnowledgeSon*). We should keep in mind that most Singles do not own a Sonite (*OwnSonite*), so this knowledge has been obtained primarily through advertising and word-of-mouth communication.

```
The message processing ability of Singles is high.
The value is high because
  the product class knowledge of Singles is high,
  and the average age of Singles is adult.

Is this acceptable (y/n)?  y
```

* With a high level of product knowledge, most Singles should be able to comprehend and respond to advertisements for Sonites. Of course, this depends on the message complexity and terminology used in the advertisement.

```
What is the performance difference from competitors of SONO?
Known values are
     1.  small
     2.  medium
     3.  large
>> small
```

* *Situation:Trend* - The actual differences between SONO and its closest competitors (SULU and SARK) are quite **small**, as shown in the following table. Both SULU and SARK are somewhat smaller, lighter, and less expensive than SONO.

	Char01 Weight	Char02 Design	Char03 Volume	Char04 Freq.	Char05 Power	Price
SONO	17	7	50	30	70	$340
SULU	15	6	40	20	70	$310
SARK	12	9	37	25	75	$325

```
What are the product category purchase motivations of Singles?
Known values are
    1.  problem removal
    2.  problem avoidance
    3.  product replacement
    4.  sensory stimulation
    5.  intellectual stimulation
    6.  social approval
    7.  self esteem
>> 4,6
```

*   *Situation:Tabulate* - Fifty percent of Singles (Cluster 1) purchase products in the Sonite category *(CategMotiv)* for **sensory stimulation**, while 40 percent purchase them for **social approval**.

```
What is the market share in this segment of SONO?
Known values are
    1.  none
    2.  small
    3.  moderate
    4.  large
>> large
```

*   *Objectives:ComAssess* - SONO has a 43.8% share of the Singles segment (Segment 2), which is **large** relative to other brands.

```
What is the performance evaluation of Sonite?
Known values are
    1.  subjective
    2.  objective
>> subjective
```

*   On the dimensions of sound quality and design, the evaluation of Sonites is largely **subjective**.

```
What is the visibility of using or the results of using SONO?
Known values are
     1.   low
     2.   high
>> low
```

* A Sonite might be used individually or in the company of others. However, the visibility of the SONO brand is **low** during use of the product.

The output of the Expert System module is shown below. ADSTRAT presents a large number of recommendations concerning possible creative strategies and communication approaches. Students should use these ideas to stimulate their own creative thinking about Sonite advertising. As noted in the student manual, ADSTRAT is a supplement and not a substitute for the creative process in ad design. Its suggestions must be combined with knowledge of the product, the target audience, the cultural environment, and competitive activities to produce effective advertising.

EXPERT SYSTEM FOR COPY DECISIONS

```
The focus of SONO ad is on brand benefits.
The value is on brand benefits because
   the ad objective of SONO is communicate brand image/mood/lifestyle.
```

```
The format of SONO ad is serious drama.
The value is serious drama because the creative strategy of SONO is
   transformational, and the message processing motivation of Singles is high.
```

```
The executional techniques for SONO ad are animation/cartoon/rotoscope, and
authentic emotional portrayal,
   and capture consumer emotions,
   and climax presentation,
   and familiar scenario,
   and fast presentation speed,
   and visual stimuli/imagery,
   and implicit conclusion,
   and music and/or singing,
   and brand name repetition,
   and many nouns in headline,
   and personal reference,
   and short headline,
```

and supporting information,
and surrogate indicators of performance,
and surrogate indicators of performance.
The value is animation/cartoon/rotoscope because the visibility in the ad of
    Power is low.
The value is authentic emotional portrayal because the creative strategy of
    SONO is transformational.
The value is capture consumer emotions because the creative strategy of SONO
    is transformational.
The value is climax presentation because the message processing motivation of
    Singles is high.
The value is familiar scenario because the creative strategy of SONO is
    transformational.
The value is fast presentation speed because the message processing ability of
    Singles is high, and the message processing motivation of Singles is high,
    and the brand performance knowledge of Singles is high.
The value is visual stimuli/imagery because the creative strategy of SONO is
    transformational.
The value is implicit conclusion because the message processing motivation of
    Singles is high.
The value is music and/or singing because the message processing ability of
    Singles is high, and the message processing motivation of Singles is high,
    and the brand performance knowledge of Singles is high.
The value is brand name repetition because the ad objective of SONO is
    maintain top-of-mind brand awareness.
The value is many nouns in headline because the ad objective of SONO is
    maintain top-of-mind brand awareness.
The value is personal reference because the ad objective of SONO is maintain
    top-of-mind brand awareness.
The value is short headline because the ad objective of SONO is maintain
    top-of-mind brand awareness.
The value is supporting information because the message processing ability of
    Singles is high, and the message processing motivation of Singles is high
The value is surrogate indicators of performance because the message
    processing ability of Singles is high, and the message processing
    motivation of Singles is high, and the performance difference from
    competitors of SONO is small.
The value is surrogate indicators of performance because the ability to judge
    product performance of Singles is low.

The recommended presenter(s) in SONO ad are likable and/or attractive, and
    likable and/or attractive, and similar to the target audience.
The value is likable and/or attractive because the decision involvement of
    Singles is high.
The value is likable and/or attractive because the creative strategy of SONO
    is transformational.

The value is similar to the target audience because the creative strategy of
   SONO is transformational, and the decision involvement of Singles is high.

The strength of claim in SONO ad is strongly positive.
The value is strongly positive because the message processing motivation of
   Singles is high, and the ability to judge product performance of Singles is
   low.

The number of benefits in SONO ad is one.
The value is one because the brand motivation direction of Singles is
positive.

The comparative approach of SONO ad is no product comparison.
The value is no product comparison because the creative strategy of SONO is
   transformational.

The argument in SONO ad is one sided brand message.
The value is one sided brand message because the creative strategy of SONO is
   transformational.

The emotional tones of SONO ad are elation and flattery.
The value is elation because the brand purchase motivation of Singles is
   sensory stimulation, and the message processing motivation of Singles is
   high.
The value is flattery because the brand purchase motivation of Singles is
   social approval, and the message processing motivation of Singles is high.

The emotional direction of SONO ad is positive.
The value is positive because the creative strategy of SONO is
transformational.

The strength of emotion in SONO ad is either weak or strong.
The value is either weak or strong because the message processing motivation
   of Singles is high.